GRADE 3

W9-AUE-430

MATH Trailblazers

A BALANCED MATHEMATICS PROGRAM INTEGRATING SCIENCE AND LANGUAGE ARTS

Discovery Assignment Book

THIRD EDITION

KENDALL/HUNT PUBLISHING COMPANY
4050 Westmark Drive   Dubuque, Iowa 52002

A TIMS® Curriculum
University of Illinois at Chicago

MATH TRAILBLAZERS®

Dedication

This book is dedicated to the children and teachers who let us see the magic in their classrooms and to our families who wholeheartedly supported us while we searched for ways to make it happen.

The TIMS Project

UIC The University of Illinois at Chicago

The original edition was based on work supported by the National Science Foundation under grant No. MDR 9050226 and the University of Illinois at Chicago. Any opinions, findings, and conclusions or recommendations expressed in this publication are those of the authors and do not necessarily reflect the views of the granting agencies.

ISBN 978-0-7575-3485-0

Printed in the United States of America

2   3   4   5   6   7   8   9   10   11   10

Table of Contents

Additional student pages may be found in the *Unit Resource Guide, Student Guide,* or the *Adventure Book.*

Table of Contents

Additional student pages may be found in the *Unit Resource Guide, Student Guide,* or the *Adventure Book.*

Table of Contents

Additional student pages may be found in the *Unit Resource Guide, Student Guide,* or the *Adventure Book.*

LETTER TO PARENTS

Dear Parents,

Math Trailblazers® is based on the ideas that mathematics is best learned through solving many different kinds of problems and that all children deserve a challenging mathematics curriculum. The program provides a careful balance of concepts and skills. Traditional arithmetic skills and procedures are covered through their repeated use in problems and through distributed practice. *Math Trailblazers,* however, offers much more. Students using this program will become proficient problem solvers, will know when and how to apply the mathematics they have  learned, and will be able to clearly communicate their mathematical knowledge. Computation, measurement, geometry, data collection and analysis, estimation, graphing, patterns and relationships, mental arithmetic, and simple algebraic ideas are all an integral part of the curriculum. They will see connections between the mathematics learned in school and the mathematics used in everyday life. And, they will enjoy and value the work they do in mathematics.

The *Discovery Assignment Book* is only one component of *Math Trailblazers.* Additional material and lessons are contained in the *Student Guide,* the *Adventure Book*, and in the teacher's *Unit Resource Guides.* If you have questions about the program, we encourage you to speak with your child's teacher.

This curriculum was built around national recommendations for improving mathematics instruction in American schools and the research that supported those recommendations. The first edition was extensively tested with thousands of children in dozens of classrooms over five years of development. In preparing the second and third editions, we have benefited from the comments and suggestions of hundreds of teachers and children who have used the curriculum. *Math Trailblazers* reflects our view of a complete and well-balanced mathematics program that will prepare children for the 21st century—a world in which mathematical skills will be important in most occupations and mathematical reasoning will be essential for acting as an informed citizen in a democratic society. We hope that you enjoy this exciting approach to learning mathematics and that you watch your child's mathematical abilities grow throughout the year.

Philip Wagreich

Philip Wagreich
Professor, Department of Mathematics, Statistics, and Computer Science
Director, Institute for Mathematics and Science Education
Teaching Integrated Mathematics and Science (TIMS) Project
University of Illinois at Chicago

Unit 1

Sampling and Classifying

	Student Guide	Discovery Assignment Book	Adventure Book	Unit Resource Guide*
Lesson 1 First Names	●	●		●
Lesson 2 Turn Over	●			
Lesson 3 Kind of Bean	●	●		●
Lesson 4 Line Math Puzzles		●		
Lesson 5 You Can't Do That			●	
Lesson 6 A Sample of Problems	●			

Unit Resource Guide pages are from the teacher materials.

Unit 1 Home Practice

PART 1

1. **A.** 4 + 7 = __11__

   B. 5 + 9 = __14__

   C. 8 + 2 + 4 = __14__

2. **A.** 10 − 4 = __6__

   B. 15 − 10 = __5__

   C. 15 − 9 = __6__

3. Carl dropped thirty-three pennies. A bunch rolled under the refrigerator. He picked up seventeen pennies. How many pennies rolled under the refrigerator? Explain how you decided.

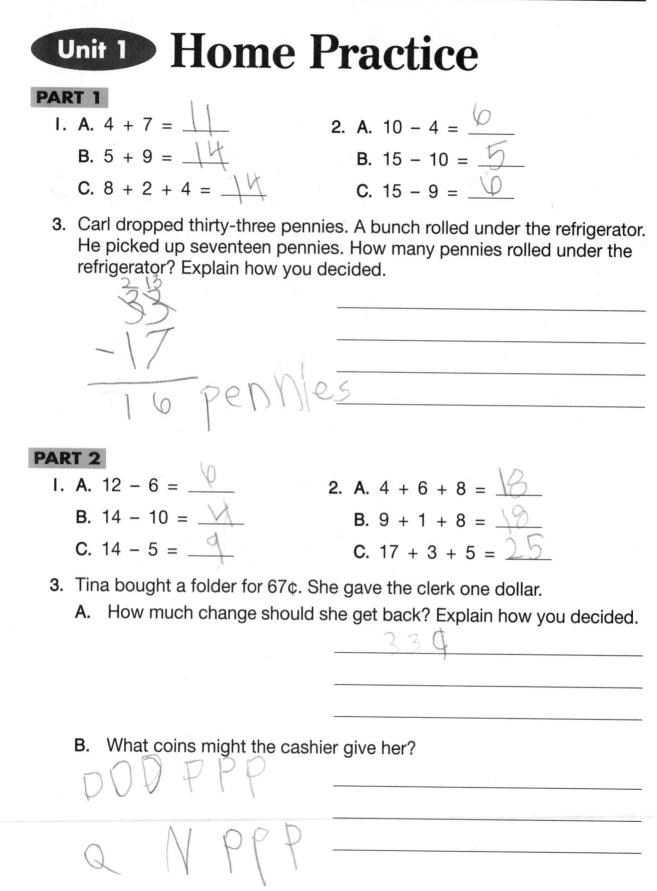

16 pennies

PART 2

1. **A.** 12 − 6 = __6__

   B. 14 − 10 = __4__

   C. 14 − 5 = __9__

2. **A.** 4 + 6 + 8 = __18__

   B. 9 + 1 + 8 = __18__

   C. 17 + 3 + 5 = __25__

3. Tina bought a folder for 67¢. She gave the clerk one dollar.

   A. How much change should she get back? Explain how you decided.

   33 ¢

   B. What coins might the cashier give her?

   DQD PPP

   Q N PPP

SAMPLING AND CLASSIFYING

Name _____ Date _____

1. Janelle's aunt just turned 34 years old. Janelle wrote the following number sentences to show how 34 can be broken into parts.

   30 + 4 = 34

   10 + 7 + 7 + 10 = 34

   Write five more number sentences that show 34 broken into parts.

   14 + 20 = 34   17 + 17 = 34   2 + 32 = 34
   10 + 10 + 10 + 2 + 2 = 34   10 + 24 = 34

2. Thirty-four is...
   A. 10 more than _24_   B. 20 + _14_
   C. 10 less than _44_   D. 100 less than _134_
   E. about half of _68_   F. about twice _17_
   G. 5 less than _39_   H. 9 more than _25_

1. It is 11:00 A.M. Alice's mom says, "You said you were going to start cleaning your room one-half hour ago." What time was Alice supposed to start cleaning?

   10:30

2. On Saturday Tim helped his dad clean the garage. It took him 20 minutes to clean each shelf. If he spent two hours cleaning the shelves, how many did he clean?

   6 shelves

Name _____ Date _9/22/20_

Sarah Diehl

First Names Data Table and Graph

Write the number of students in each row in the table. Use the table to make a bar graph.

L Number of Letters	S Number of Students
1	0
2	0
3	1
4	2
5	5
6	3
7	0
8	0
9	0
10	0
11	0

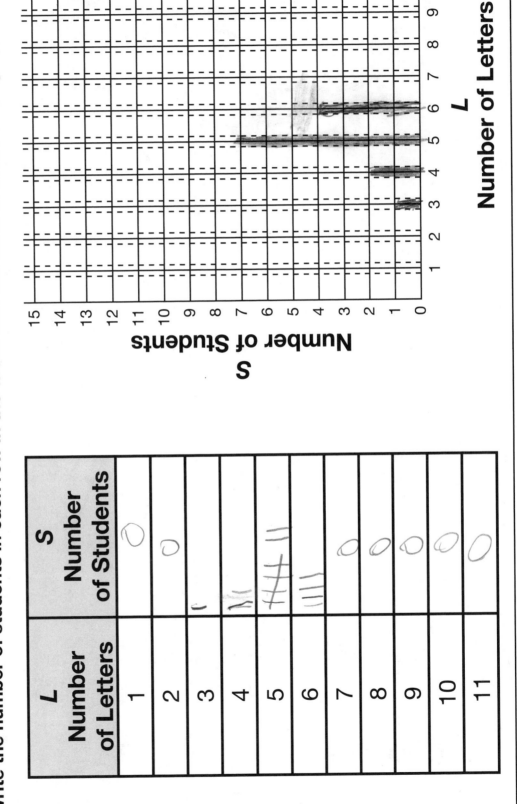

First Names

DAB • Grade 3 • Unit 1 • Lesson 1   **5**

Family Names Data Table

Homework

Dear Family Member:

Help your child collect at least ten first names from your immediate or extended family. Write each family member's name in the Names of Family Members column next to the number of letters in the name. For example, "James" would be written in the row with "5."

Thank you for your cooperation.

Collect at least ten first names from your family. Write them in the correct row.

Family Names

L Number of Letters in the First Name	Names of Family Members
1	
2	
3	Tim, Zoe
4	
5	sarah, Devin
6	Debbie, Hannah, caylee
7	Zachary
8	Rhiannah
9	
10	
11	

Family Names Graph

🎒Homework

Dear Family Member:

In class, we collected data on the number of letters in our first names. We displayed this data in a bar graph. Now, your child is using the data from your *Family Names Data Table* to create a new bar graph. Ask your child how this graph compares to the graph made in school.

Thank you for your help.

Graph the data from your *Family Names Data Table*. Use the labels on the graph to help you. Use the dotted lines to help you draw the bars.

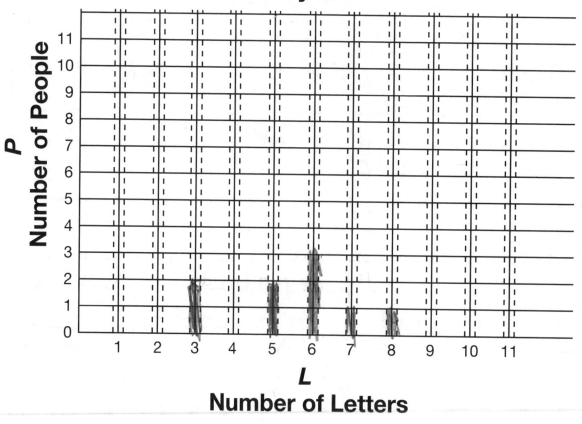

Family Names

P — Number of People

L — Number of Letters

Name ___Sarah___ Date ___9/29/20___

Kind of Bean

Use the TIMS Laboratory Method to investigate the population of beans.

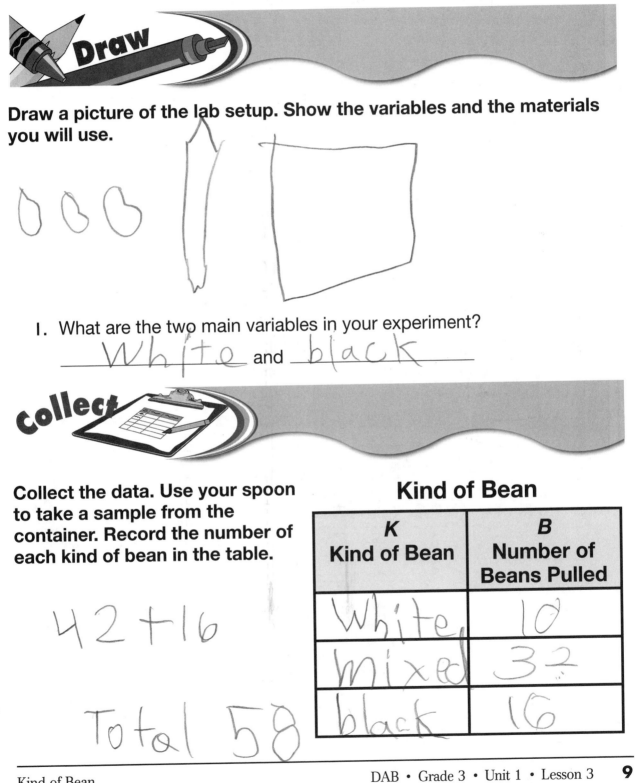

Draw

Draw a picture of the lab setup. Show the variables and the materials you will use.

1. What are the two main variables in your experiment?
   ___White___ and ___black___

Collect

Collect the data. Use your spoon to take a sample from the container. Record the number of each kind of bean in the table.

42 + 16

Total 58

Kind of Bean

K Kind of Bean	B Number of Beans Pulled
White	10
mixed	32
black	16

Graph

Make a bar graph of your results. Remember to label the graph.

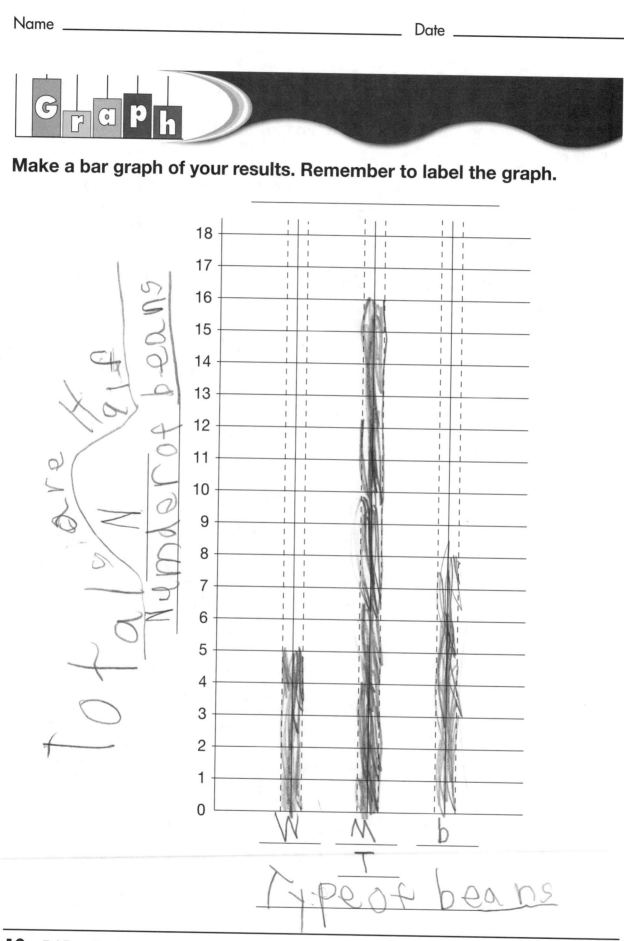

Kind of Bean

Answer the following questions using your data table and graph.

2. A. What kind of bean was most common in your sample?

    _____

    B. How many did you have of this kind of bean? _____

3. A. What kind of bean was least common in your sample? _____

    B. How many did you have of this kind of bean? _____

4. What was the total number of beans in your sample? _____

5. Explain how you found the answer to Question 4.

    _____

    _____

    _____

    _____

    _____

6. You are going to collect a second sample.

    A. Predict which kind of bean will be the most common.

    _____

    B. Which kind of bean will be the least common?

    _____

    C. Explain how you decided on your answers.

    _____

    _____

    _____

    _____

7. Take a second sample. Count the beans and record your data in the table.

Second Sample

K Kind of Bean	B Number of Beans Pulled

8. Were your predictions correct? Why or why not?

_____

_____

9. Suppose you used a much larger scoop to take a sample.

A. How would the data in your data table change?

_____

_____

_____

_____

B. How would your graph change?

_____

_____

_____

_____

10. Use your data to make predictions about the bean population (all of the beans in your container). Predict which bean is the most common and which bean is the least common. Tell why you think so. Write your answers on a separate sheet of paper.

Kind of Bean

Toni's Candy Grab

🎒 Homework

Dear Family Member:

Your child is learning to represent data in a bar graph. Check to see that your child's graph matches the data in Toni's table and that the graph is properly labeled.

Thank you.

Toni took one sample of candies from a brown bag. This is her data:

Toni's Data

C Color	N Number of Candies Pulled
red	6
green	2
blue	2

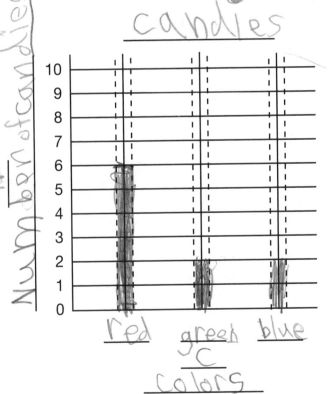

1. How many candies did she grab in one handful?

   __10__

2. Graph her data. Remember to give the graph a title.

Line Math Puzzles 1

Cut out the digits in the boxes below and use them to help solve the puzzles.

Put 1, 2, 3, 4, and 5 in the boxes so that the sum of each line is 9.

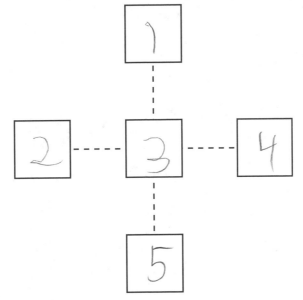

Put 5, 6, 7, 8, and 9 in the boxes so that the sum of each line is 21.

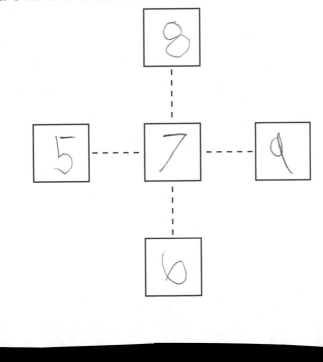

Line Math Puzzles 2

Cut out the digits in the boxes below and use them to help solve the puzzles.

Put 1, 2, 3, 4, 5, 6, and 7 in the boxes so that the sum of each line is 12.

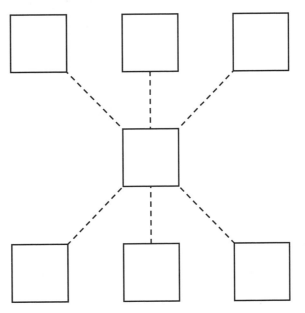

Put 1, 2, 3, 7, 8, and 9 in the boxes so that the sum of each line is 12.

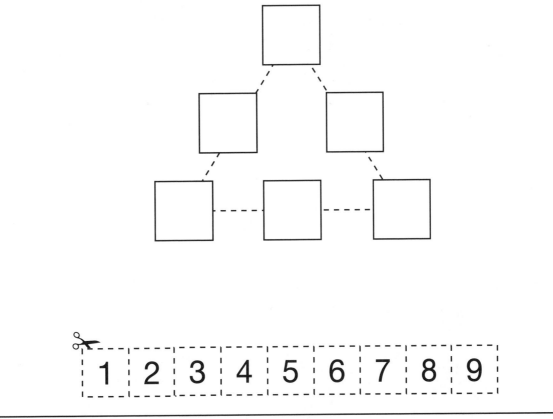

| 1 | 2 | 3 | 4 | 5 | 6 | 7 | 8 | 9 |

Your Own Line Math Puzzle

Dear Family Member:

Please help your child make line puzzles where each row adds up to the same sum.

Thank you for your cooperation.

Make up your own line math puzzle using the steps below.

1. Choose one of these three designs to use for your puzzle. Copy it onto another piece of paper.

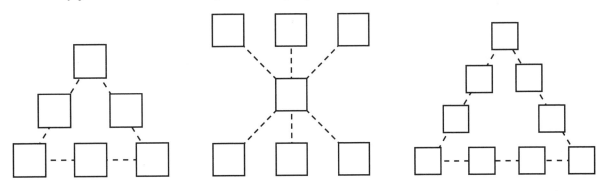

2. Use numbers less than ten to solve the puzzle so that the sum of each line is the same. *Any digit can be used more than once.*

3. Write the digits in the boxes. This will be the answer key for your puzzle. Check that all the line sums are the same.

4. Write down the sum and the digits that are needed to solve the puzzle. If you use a digit more than once, make sure you write that digit as many times as you used it.

5. Give the puzzle to a friend to solve. Check your friend's work, and fix your puzzle if it has a mistake.

6. Make a clean copy of your puzzle and key. Turn in all your work to your teacher.

Unit 2

Strategies: An Assessment Unit

	Student Guide	Discovery Assignment Book	Adventure Book	Unit Resource Guide*
Lesson 1				
Addition Facts Strategies	●	●		●
Lesson 2				
Spinning Sums	●	●		
Lesson 3				
Yü the Great A Chinese Legend			●	
Lesson 4				
Magic Squares	●	●		
Lesson 5				
Subtraction Facts Strategies	●	●		
Lesson 6				
Spinning Differences				●
Lesson 7				
Assessing the Subtraction Facts		●		
Lesson 8				
Number Sense with Dollars and Cents	●			

Unit Resource Guide pages are from the teacher materials.

21

Unit 2 Home Practice

PART 1

I. A. 18 − 10 = __8__   2. A. 4 + 4 + 8 = __16__

   B. 13 − 6 = __7__   B. 7 + 9 + 8 = __24__

   C. 14 − 9 = __5__   C. 15 + 7 + 4 = __26__

3. Kyle received eight new books for his birthday. He now has fifty-two books. How many books did Kyle have before his birthday? Show how you found your answer.

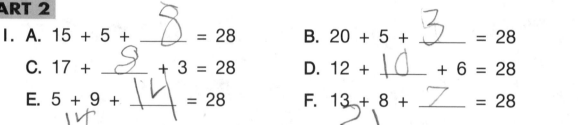

$52 - 8 = 44$

_____

_____

_____

_____

PART 2

I. A. 15 + 5 + __8__ = 28   B. 20 + 5 + __3__ = 28

   C. 17 + __8__ + 3 = 28   D. 12 + __10__ + 6 = 28

   E. 5 + 9 + __14__ = 28   F. 13 + 8 + __7__ = 28

   14   21

2. For the food drive, Ron's class collected seventeen cans of vegetables, four cans of fruit, and nine cans of soup.

   A.   How many cans did they collect?

   17   _____

                               _____

   B.   How many more cans of vegetables are there than soup?

                               _____

                               _____

STRATEGIES: AN ASSESSMENT UNIT

Name _____ Date _____

PART 3

1. Does your kitchen table have square corners? How did you decide?

   _____

   _____

   _____

2. Make a list of square-cornered objects that are in your home.

   _____

   _____

   _____

PART 4

You go to the store to buy supplies. The prices are listed below. Explain your thinking for each problem.

eraser	30¢	folder	67¢
pencil	17¢	box of crayons	89¢
ruler	49¢	marker	42¢

1. You have one dollar. Can you buy a box of crayons and a pencil?

   _____

   _____

2. You have one dollar. Can you buy one marker, one folder, and a ruler?

   _____

   _____

   _____

3. Your friend has $2. What can he or she buy?

   _____

   _____

   _____

Switch It!

1. Complete the following problems in your head. Try to use a ten whenever possible. Choose two problems and tell how you solved each one. You can use pictures, words, or number sentences.

   A. 3 + 16 + 7 = _____

   B. 9 + 17 + 1 = _____

   C. 2 + 11 + 8 = _____

   D. 5 + 15 + 6 = _____

   E. 7 + 12 + 8 = _____

2. Write and solve your own addition problem.

Calculator Explorations

Homework

Dear Family Member:

Please help your child complete the problems below without a calculator. This work will be checked with calculators in class. Encourage your child to look for tens. For example, $7 + 16 + 4$ could be solved by pressing: [7] [+] [3] [+] [13] [+] [4] [=] . Ask your child which addends make a ten.

Thank you for your help.

Imagine the six key on your calculator is broken. What keystrokes would you press to do the problems below? Look for tens. List your keystrokes and write the sum. You do not have to fill all the boxes.

1. $6 + 15 + 2 =$ _____

2. $17 + 6 + 4 =$ _____

3. $14 + 6 + 7 =$ _____

4. $6 + 18 + 1 =$ _____

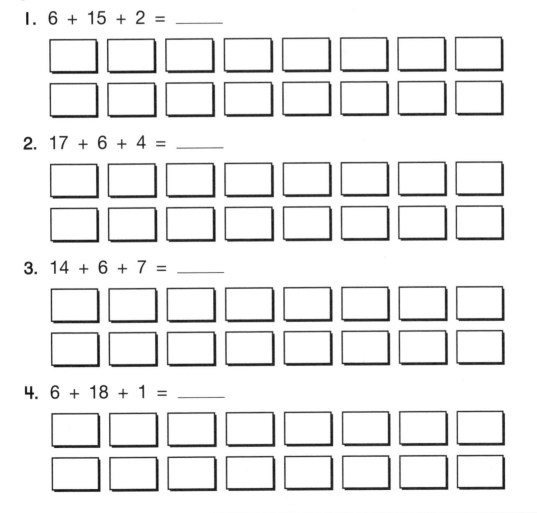

Spinners 2–9

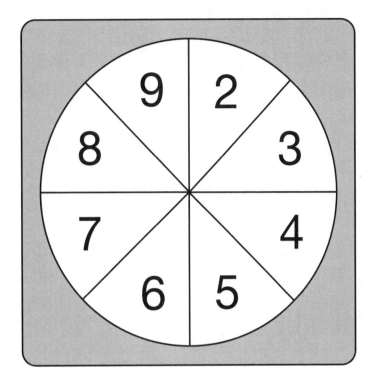

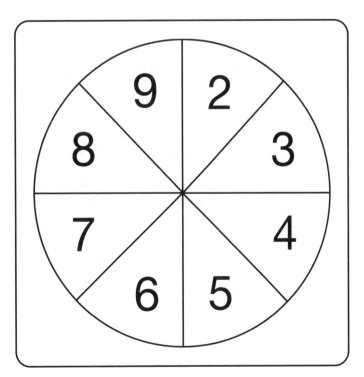

Spinning Sums Data Table

Spinning Sums Data Table

Sum	Number Sentence	How Many?

Digits

Cut out these digits to help you solve magic squares.

2	2	2	4	4	4	6	6	6

Use the following digits for Question 3 in your *Student Guide*.

3	3	3	5	5	5	7	7	7

Use the following digits for Question 4 in your *Student Guide*.

1	1	1	5	5	5	9	9	9

Use the following digits for homework Question 1.

3	3	3	6	6	6	9	9	9

Use the following digits for homework Questions 2 and 3.

6	7	8	9	10	11	12	13	14
15								

Spinners 11–18 and 9–10

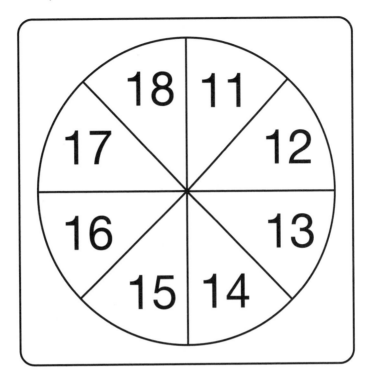

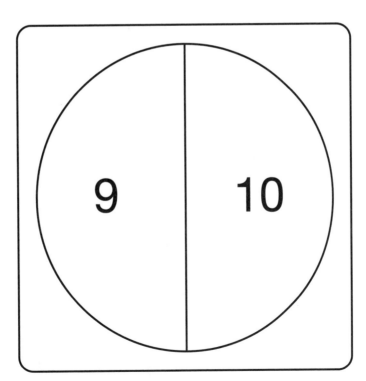

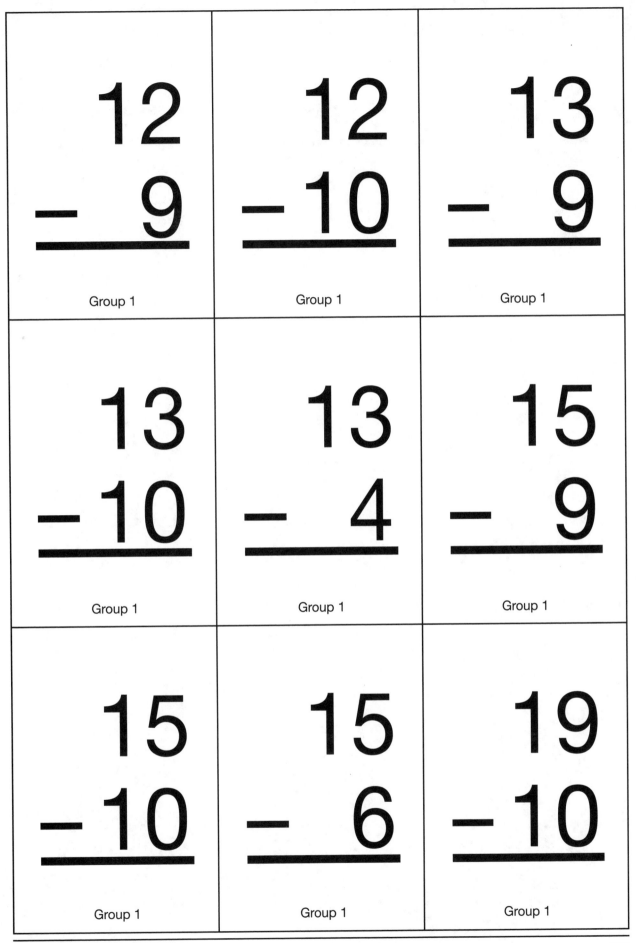

$$\begin{array}{r} 12 \\ -\ 9 \\ \hline \end{array}$$

Group 1

$$\begin{array}{r} 12 \\ -10 \\ \hline \end{array}$$

Group 1

$$\begin{array}{r} 13 \\ -\ 9 \\ \hline \end{array}$$

Group 1

$$\begin{array}{r} 13 \\ -10 \\ \hline \end{array}$$

Group 1

$$\begin{array}{r} 13 \\ -\ 4 \\ \hline \end{array}$$

Group 1

$$\begin{array}{r} 15 \\ -\ 9 \\ \hline \end{array}$$

Group 1

$$\begin{array}{r} 15 \\ -10 \\ \hline \end{array}$$

Group 1

$$\begin{array}{r} 15 \\ -\ 6 \\ \hline \end{array}$$

Group 1

$$\begin{array}{r} 19 \\ -10 \\ \hline \end{array}$$

Group 1

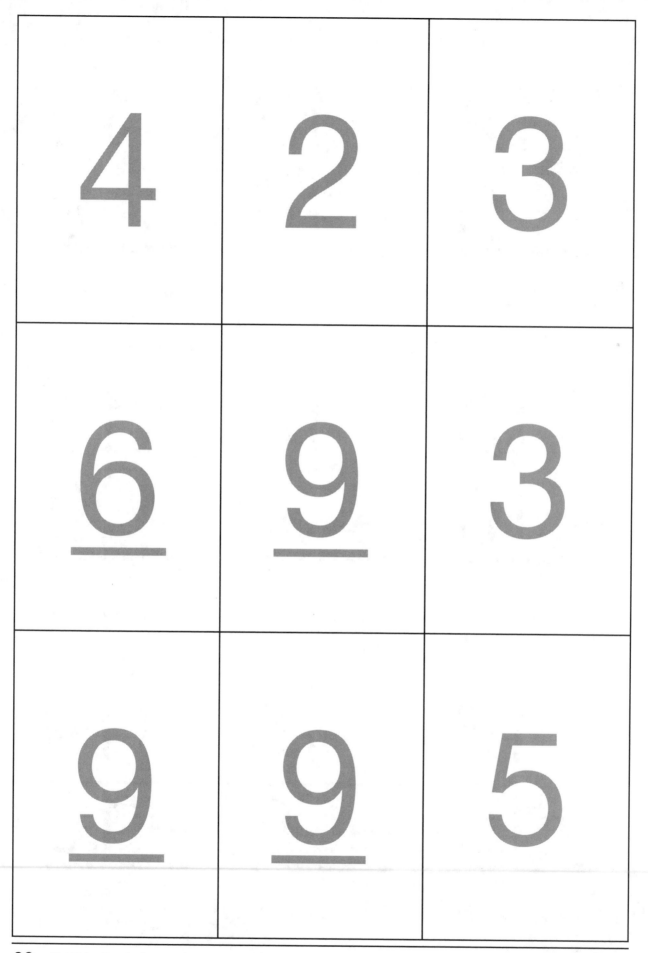

Assessing the Subtraction Facts

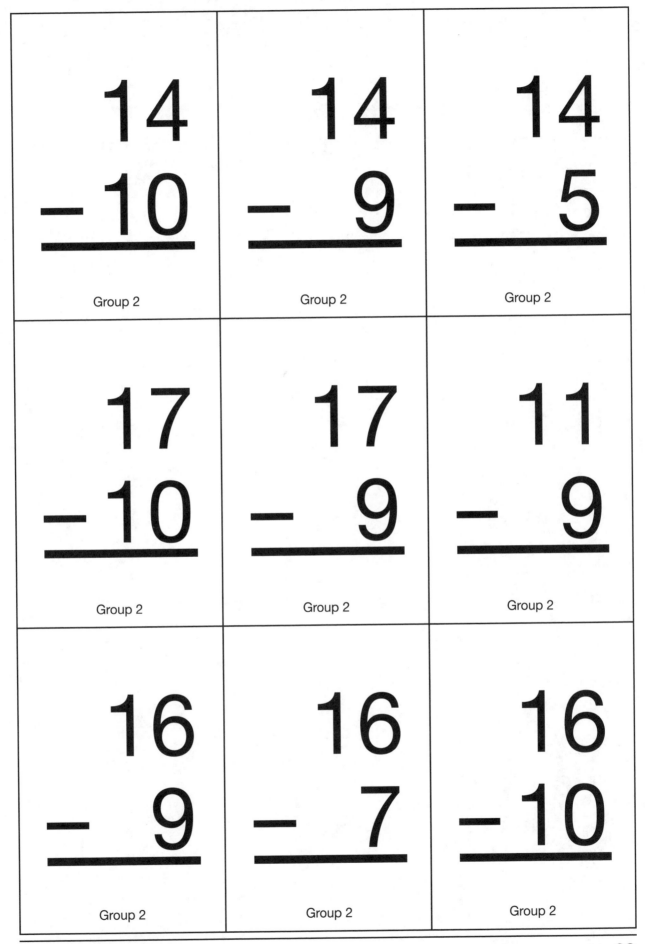

Assessing the Subtraction Facts

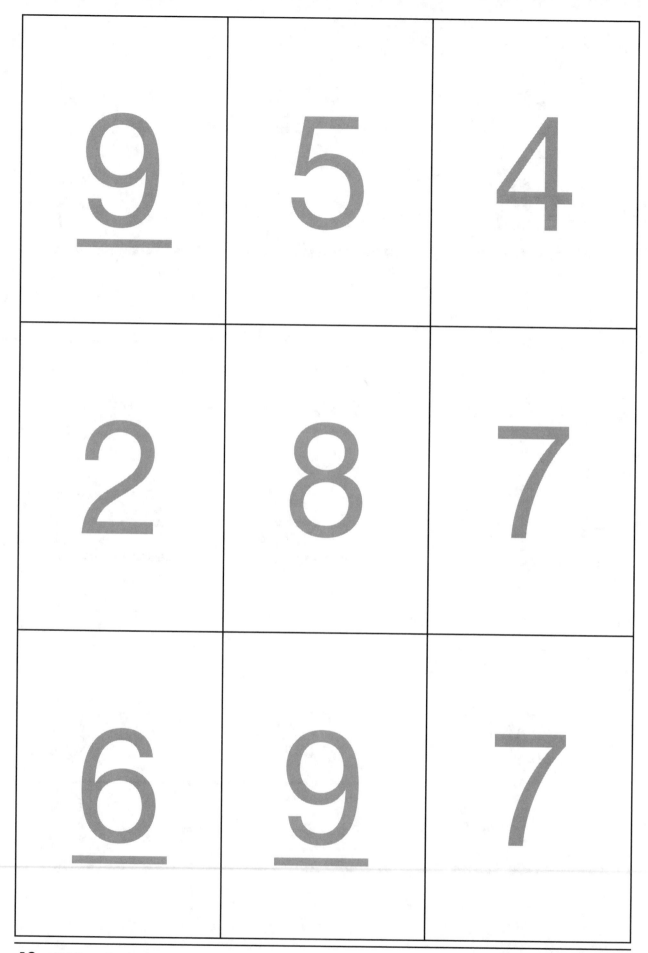

Name _____

Date _____

Sorting Flash Cards

Problems Answered Correctly and Quickly	Problems Answered Correctly after Thinking	Problems Answered Incorrectly

Name _____ Date _____

Subtraction Facts I Know

Circle the subtraction facts you know and can answer quickly.
Underline those facts that you know when you use a strategy.
Do nothing to those facts that you still need to learn.

4 − 2 2	5 − 2 3	6 − 2 4	7 − 2 5	8 − 2 6	9 − 2 7	10 − 2 8	11 − 2 9
5 − 3 2	6 − 3 3	7 − 3 4	8 − 3 5	9 − 3 6	10 − 3 7	11 − 3 8	12 − 3 9
6 − 4 2	7 − 4 3	8 − 4 4	9 − 4 5	10 − 4 6	11 − 4 7	12 − 4 8	13 − 4 9
7 − 5 2	8 − 5 3	9 − 5 4	10 − 5 5	11 − 5 6	12 − 5 7	13 − 5 8	14 − 5 9
8 − 6 2	9 − 6 3	10 − 6 4	11 − 6 5	12 − 6 6	13 − 6 7	14 − 6 8	15 − 6 9
9 − 7 2	10 − 7 3	11 − 7 4	12 − 7 5	13 − 7 6	14 − 7 7	15 − 7 8	16 − 7 9
10 − 8 2	11 − 8 3	12 − 8 4	13 − 8 5	14 − 8 6	15 − 8 7	16 − 8 8	17 − 8 9
11 − 9 2	12 − 9 3	13 − 9 4	14 − 9 5	15 − 9 6	16 − 9 7	17 − 9 8	18 − 9 9
12 − 10 2	13 − 10 3	14 − 10 4	15 − 10 5	16 − 10 6	17 − 10 7	18 − 10 8	19 − 10 9

Unit 3

Exploring Multiplication

	Student Guide	Discovery Assignment Book	Adventure Book	Unit Resource Guide*
Lesson 1				
T-Shirt Factory Problems	●			
Lesson 2				
In Twos, Threes, and More	●	●		
Lesson 3				
Multiplication Stories	●			
Lesson 4				
Making Teams		●		
Lesson 5				
Multiples on the Calendar				●
Lesson 6				
More T-Shirt Problems	●			

Unit Resource Guide pages are from the teacher materials.

Name _____ Date _____

Unit 3 Home Practice

PART 1

1. A. $9 - 5 =$ _____

   B. $11 - 7 =$ _____

   C. $10 - 2 =$ _____

2. A. $90 - 50 =$ _____

   B. $110 - 70 =$ _____

   C. $100 - 20 =$ _____

3. When the school bus arrived at school, Carla counted the number of people on it. There were twenty-four people. This was sixteen more than when she first got on. How many people were on the bus when Carla got on?

   _____

   _____

   _____

   _____

PART 2

Five third-grade students are competing in a math contest. They each bought a shirt with "math" printed on the front. Show how you solved the problem.

1. How many letters were printed in all?

   _____

   _____

   _____

2. If each letter costs 10¢, how much did it cost to have "math" printed on all five shirts?

   _____

   _____

   _____

PART 3

1. A. 60 + 40 = _____

   B. 80 + 30 = _____

   C. 70 + 90 = _____

2. A. 17 + 9 = _____

   B. 15 + 8 = _____

   C. 25 + 7 = _____

3. Bob saved $42 from allowances and birthday gifts. His sister said, "You saved seven more dollars than I did." How much did Bob's sister save?

   _____

   _____

   _____

   _____

PART 4

1. Write a story and draw a picture about 10 × 9. Write a number sentence about your picture.

2. You have twenty-seven stickers to share among four friends. How many stickers does each friend get? Draw a picture and use a number sentence to show how you decided.

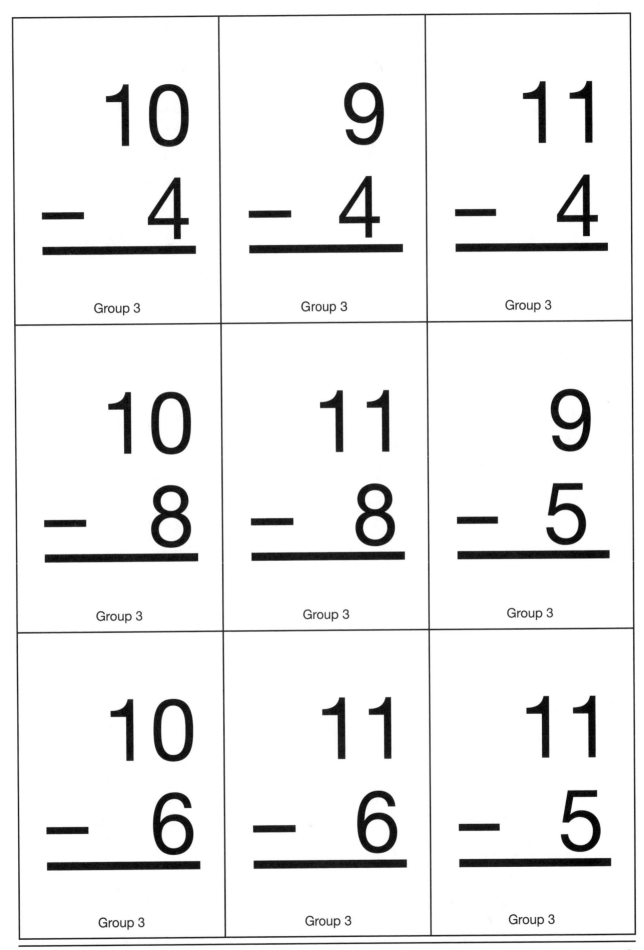

$\begin{array}{r}10\\-\ 4\\\hline\end{array}$	$\begin{array}{r}9\\-\ 4\\\hline\end{array}$	$\begin{array}{r}11\\-\ 4\\\hline\end{array}$
Group 3	Group 3	Group 3
$\begin{array}{r}10\\-\ 8\\\hline\end{array}$	$\begin{array}{r}11\\-\ 8\\\hline\end{array}$	$\begin{array}{r}9\\-\ 5\\\hline\end{array}$
Group 3	Group 3	Group 3
$\begin{array}{r}10\\-\ 6\\\hline\end{array}$	$\begin{array}{r}11\\-\ 6\\\hline\end{array}$	$\begin{array}{r}11\\-\ 5\\\hline\end{array}$
Group 3	Group 3	Group 3

EXPLORING MULTIPLICATION

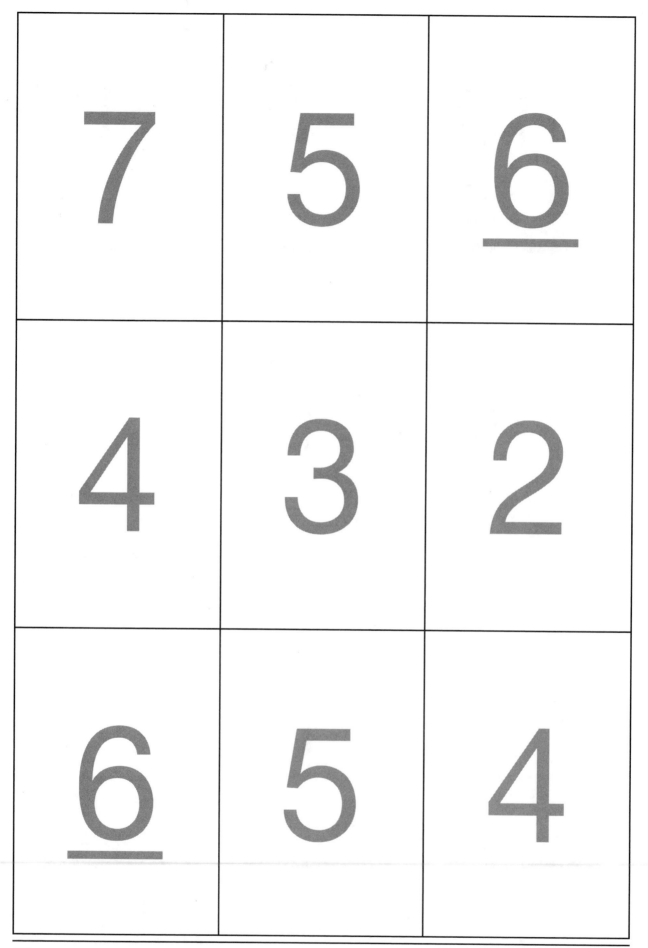

EXPLORING MULTIPLICATION

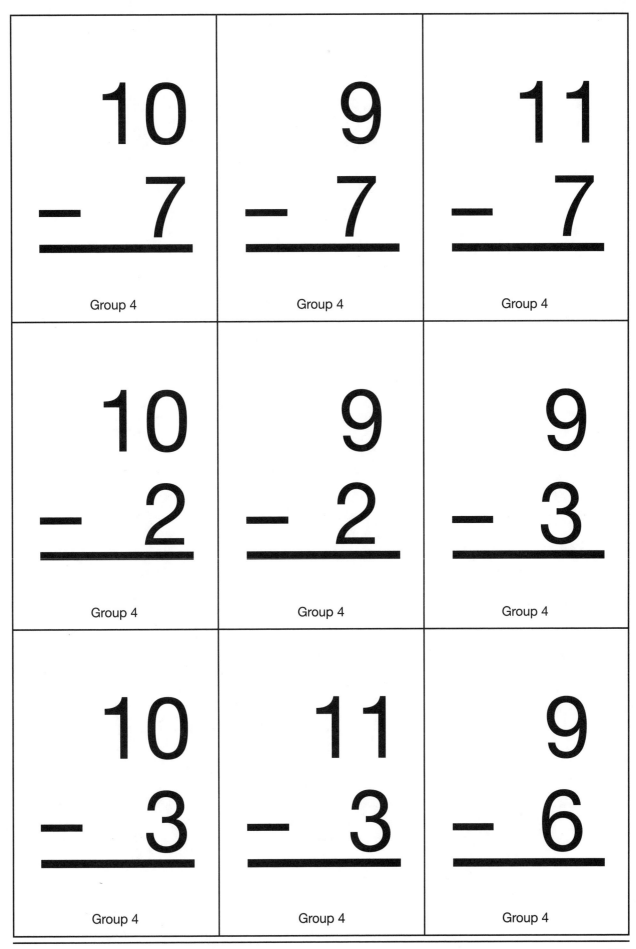

10 − 7 Group 4	9 − 7 Group 4	11 − 7 Group 4
10 − 2 Group 4	9 − 2 Group 4	9 − 3 Group 4
10 − 3 Group 4	11 − 3 Group 4	9 − 6 Group 4

EXPLORING MULTIPLICATION

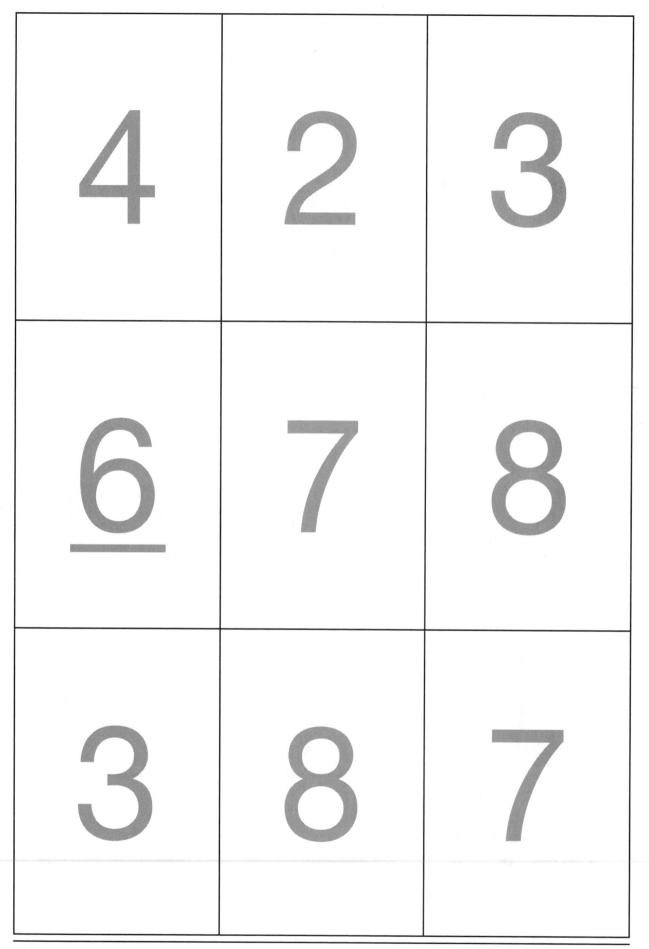

EXPLORING MULTIPLICATION

In Twos through Twelves

Homework

Dear Family Member:

We are working with things that come in groups. For example, wheels on a bicycle come in groups of two. You can help by suggesting other items that come in groups. Then have your child fill in as much of the table as he or she can.

Thank you.

List things that come in:

Groups of	Examples	Groups of	Examples
Twos		Eights	
Threes		Nines	
Fours		Tens	
Fives		Elevens	
Sixes		Twelves	
Sevens			

Class Teams Table

Record your class size and complete the data table.

Class size _____

Number of Teams	Team Size	Remainder	Number Sentence

Name ___Sarah___   Date ___10/7/20___

Groupings and Number Sentences for Ten

Homework

Dear Family Member:

Help your child fill in the missing drawings and numbers that describe how to group ten in ones, twos, threes, fours, fives, and sixes. Then help your child write the matching number sentences.

Thank you for your cooperation.

Draw groups and write number sentences to complete the data table.

Group Size	Drawings and Words	Number Sentence
1	✳ ✳ ✳ ✳ ✳ ✳ ✳ ✳ ✳ ✳ 10 groups of 1 with 0 extra	$10 \times 1 = 10$
2	✳✳ ✳✳ ✳✳ ✳✳ ✳✳ 5 groups of 2 with 0 extra	$5 \times 2 = 10$
3	✳✳✳ ✳✳✳ ✳✳✳ ✳ 3 groups of 3 with 1 extra	$3 \times 3 + 1 = 10$
4	XXXX XXXX XX _2_ groups of 4 with _2_ extra	$2 \times 4 + 2 = 10$
5	XXXXX XXXXX _2_ groups of 5 with _0_ extra	$2 \times 5 + 0 = 10$
6	XXXXXX XXXX _1_ groups of 6 with _4_ extra	$1 \times 6 + 4 = 10$

The game *Jacks* is played with ten jacks, which are small metal stars. A player throws a small ball into the air, picks up one jack, and catches the ball before it bounces twice. The player continues, picking up one jack at a time until all 10 jacks have been picked up. If successful, the player picks up groups of two, three, and so on. The first person to complete all group sizes is the winner.

Groupings and Number Sentences for Fifteen

Homework

Fill in the missing drawings, numbers, and number sentences. You will be working with fifteen as the total.

Group Size	Drawings and Words	Number Sentence
1	✳ ✳ ✳ ✳ ✳ ✳ ✳ ✳ ✳ ✳ ✳ ✳ ✳ ✳ ✳ 15 groups of 1 with 0 extra	$15 \times 1 =$ ___
2	✳✳ ✳✳ ✳✳ ✳✳ ✳✳ ✳✳ ✳✳ ✳ ___ groups of 2 with ___ extra	___ $\times 2 + 1 = 15$
3	✳✳✳ ✳✳✳ ✳✳✳ ✳✳✳ ✳✳✳ ___ groups of 3 with ___ extra	___ $\times 3 +$ ___ $= 15$
4	 ___ groups of 4 with ___ extra	___ $\times 4 +$ ___ $= 15$
5	 ___ groups of 5 with ___ extra	
6	 ___ groups of 6 with ___ extra	
7	 ___ groups of 7 with ___ extra	
8	 ___ groups of 8 with ___ extra	

Place Value Concepts

	Student Guide	Discovery Assignment Book	Adventure Book	Unit Resource Guide*
Lesson 1				
Breaking Numbers into Parts		●		●
Lesson 2				
The TIMS Candy Company	●	●		●
Lesson 3				
Base-Ten Addition	●	●		
Lesson 4				
Bubble Sort				
Lesson 5				
It's Time	●	●		●
Lesson 6				
Time for Problems	●			

Unit Resource Guide pages are from the teacher materials.

Unit 4 Home Practice

1. **A.** 12 − 4 = _____   2. **A.** 3 + 8 = _____

   B. 52 − 4 = _____   **B.** 43 + 8 = _____

   C. 72 − 4 = _____   **C.** 123 + 8 = _____

3. Alicia's class has 34 students in it. Draw a picture to show how many teams of four can be formed. Write a number sentence to describe this problem.

4. **A.** Skip count by tens from 100 to 300.

   _____

   B. Skip count by hundreds from 100 to 1000.

   _____

PART 2

1. **A.** 80 − 20 = _____   2. **A.** 110 − 20 = _____

   B. 30 + 40 = _____   **B.** 30 + 90 = _____

   C. 50 − 30 = _____   **C.** 130 − 50 = _____

3. Break the following numbers into two, three, or four parts.

   A. 79 = _____ + _____

   B. 507 = _____ + _____

   507 = _____ + _____ + _____

   C. 1551 = _____ + _____ + _____

   1551 = _____ + _____ + _____ + _____

PLACE VALUE CONCEPTS

PART 3

1. Use base-ten shorthand to represent the following numbers:

   A. 76   **B.** 29

2. Riley counted 76 red cars while driving to the shopping mall with his dad. He counted 29 red cars on the way back home. How many red cars did he count? Show how you solved the problem.

3. Solve the problem a second way. Show your second method.

PART 4

1. Erin works part-time at the TIMS Candy Company. She punches in at 8 A.M. and punches out at 11:30 A.M. How many hours does she work?

   _____

2. **A.** Jayne has 7 dimes and 25 pennies. How much money does she

      have? _____

   B. If she traded the pennies for as many dimes as possible, how many dimes would she have in all?

      _____

   C. How many pennies would be left over? _____

3. Nathan has 3 dollars, 2 dimes, and 7 pennies. If he trades his money for all pennies, how many pennies will he have?

   _____

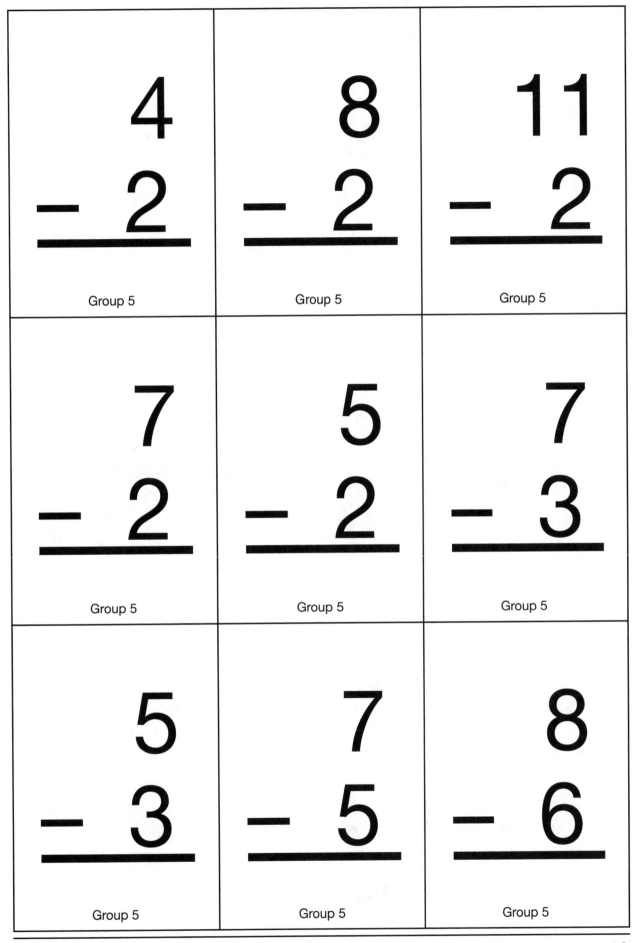

$$\begin{array}{r} 4 \\ -\ 2 \\ \hline \end{array}$$

Group 5

$$\begin{array}{r} 8 \\ -\ 2 \\ \hline \end{array}$$

Group 5

$$\begin{array}{r} 11 \\ -\ 2 \\ \hline \end{array}$$

Group 5

$$\begin{array}{r} 7 \\ -\ 2 \\ \hline \end{array}$$

Group 5

$$\begin{array}{r} 5 \\ -\ 2 \\ \hline \end{array}$$

Group 5

$$\begin{array}{r} 7 \\ -\ 3 \\ \hline \end{array}$$

Group 5

$$\begin{array}{r} 5 \\ -\ 3 \\ \hline \end{array}$$

Group 5

$$\begin{array}{r} 7 \\ -\ 5 \\ \hline \end{array}$$

Group 5

$$\begin{array}{r} 8 \\ -\ 6 \\ \hline \end{array}$$

Group 5

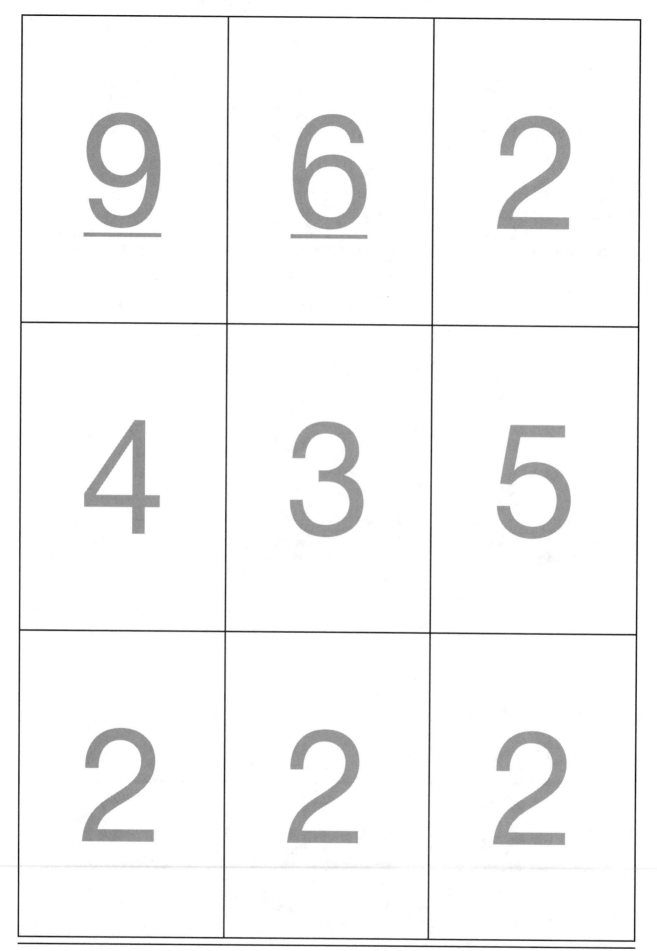

PLACE VALUE CONCEPTS

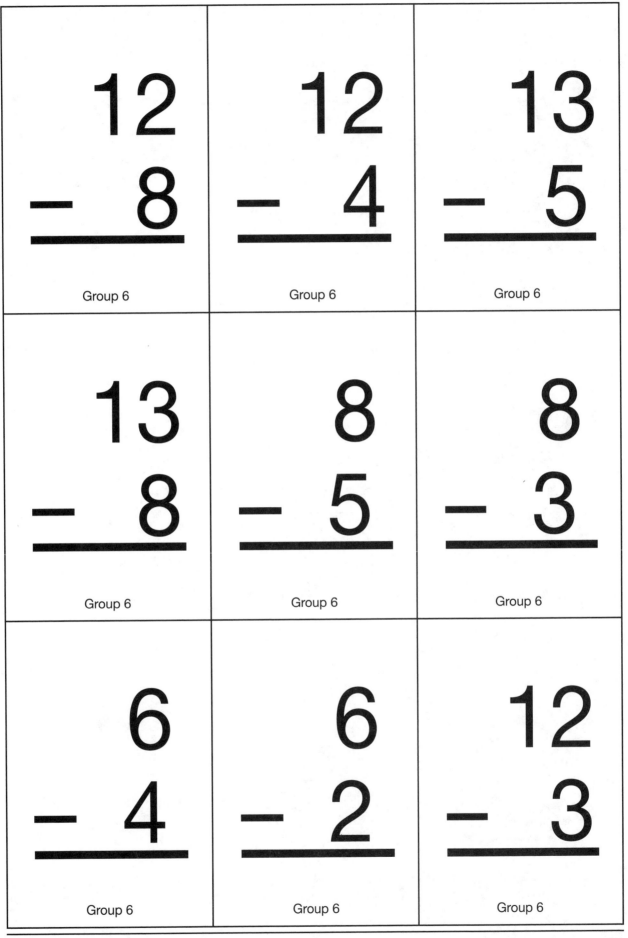

12 − 8	12 − 4	13 − 5
Group 6	Group 6	Group 6
13 − 8	8 − 5	8 − 3
Group 6	Group 6	Group 6
6 − 4	6 − 2	12 − 3
Group 6	Group 6	Group 6

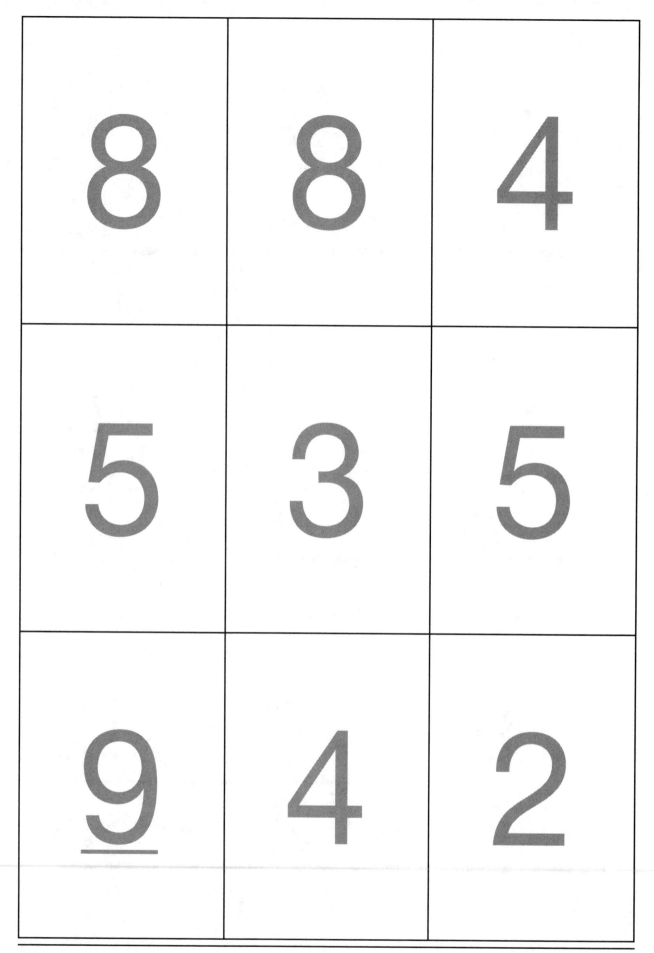

PLACE VALUE CONCEPTS

Pack 'Em Up!

Help Eric keep track of the Chocos he made at the TIMS Candy Company. In each problem, circle the bits Eric can snap together to make skinnies. Draw the skinnies in the skinnies column. Then, record the skinnies and bits on Eric's Recording Sheet. The first one is done for you.

1.

Eric's Recording Sheet

	16
1	6

2.

Eric's Recording Sheet

	25

3.

Eric's Recording Sheet

4.

Eric's Recording Sheet

Professor Peabody was helping pack Chocos at the TIMS Candy Company. He wrote the different ways he could pack the Chocos on the Recording Sheet. Some of the numbers were written with invisible ink. Help the TIMS Candy Company fill in the missing numbers. The first one is done for you.

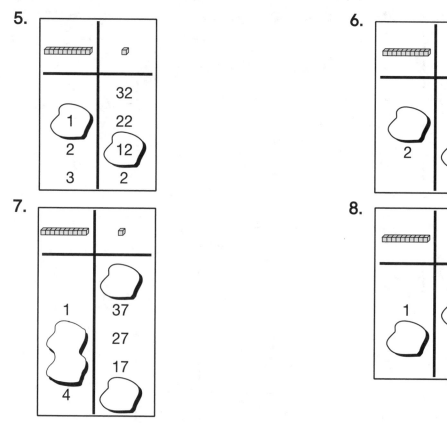

5.

🟫	🔲
	32
1	22
2	12
3	2

6.

🟫	🔲
	24
	14
2	

7.

🟫	🔲
1	37
	27
	17
4	

8.

🟫	🔲
	29
1	
	9

9. Alissa made 43 Chocos. She wrote down all the different ways 43 Chocos can be recorded.

🟫	🔲
	43
1	33
2	23
3	13
4	3

Which way uses the Fewest Pieces Rule? _____

10. Sam said, "The different ways Alissa recorded the Chocos are partitions of 43, which is 1 skinny and 33 bits. Since a skinny has 10 bits, this is like saying 10 + 33. You can show this partition of 43 as 10 + 33 = 43." Show the other partitions on Alissa's Recording Sheet using number sentences.

_____

_____

11. Show all the different ways you can put 27 cubes on the *Base-Ten Board Part 1* on the following recording sheet. Write number sentences showing the partitions.

_____

_____

_____

12. Show all the different ways you can put 45 cubes on the *Base-Ten Board Part 1* on the following recording sheet. Write number sentences showing the partitions.

_____

_____

_____

_____

_____

The Company Pays Its Bills

The TIMS Candy Company pays many bills. When writing a check, the amount is written in numbers and in words.

Here is a check for $502.00 to the Cocoa Supply Company.

TIMS Candy Company
555 E. Main Street
Chicago, IL 60600

109

June 8, 2004

PAY TO THE ORDER OF ___ Cocoa Supply Company ___ $ 502.00

Five hundred two ___ DOLLARS

Integrated Federal Bank

Memo ___

Tim Jones

Help the TIMS Candy Company by writing checks to the following companies.

1. Sugary Sweet Sugar Company for $487.00.

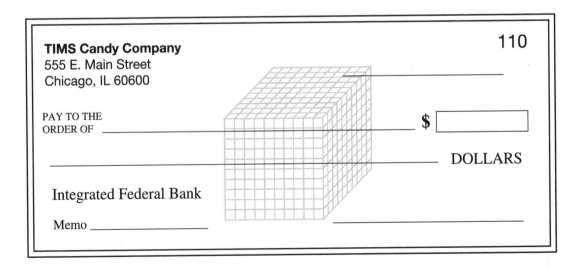

TIMS Candy Company
555 E. Main Street
Chicago, IL 60600

110

PAY TO THE ORDER OF ___ $ ___

___ DOLLARS

Integrated Federal Bank

Memo ___

2. Recycled Paper Company for $105.00.

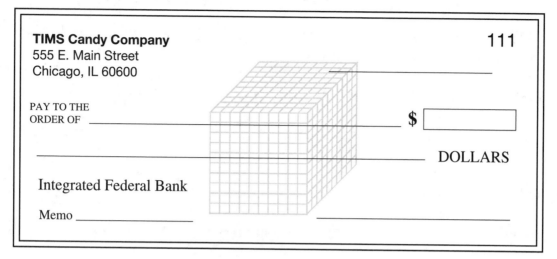

3. Box-It-Up Cardboard Company for $1006.00.

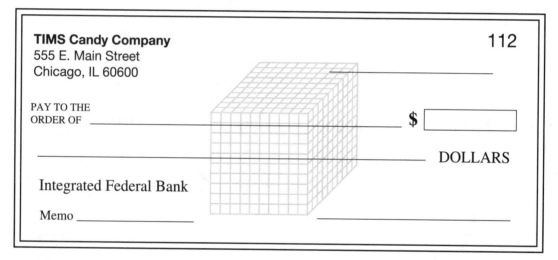

4. Bovine Dairy for $677.00.

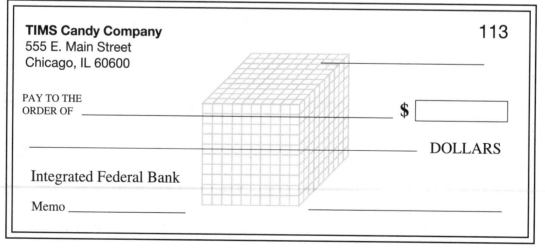

Name _____ Date _____

Getting to Know Base-Ten Shorthand

1. Eric used base-ten shorthand to show the Chocos he made. How many Chocos did Eric make?

   A. _____

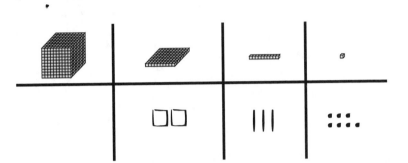

   B. _____

2. Alissa made 254 Chocos. Draw this amount using base-ten shorthand.

The TIMS Candy Company   DAB • Grade 3 • Unit 4 • Lesson 2   **73**

3. Professor Peabody forgot to use the *Base-Ten Board* when he drew the Chocos he made at the TIMS Candy Company. Figure out how many Chocos Professor Peabody made.

A.    _____

B.   _____

4. Professor Peabody forgot to use the Fewest Pieces Rule to record his Chocos. Correct Professor Peabody's work by drawing the amount using the Fewest Pieces Rule. Write down how many Chocos were made.

A.   _____

B.   _____

C.   _____

Shortcut Addition

Solve each of the addition problems below using base-ten shorthand.
Then, solve the problem using the shortcut method.

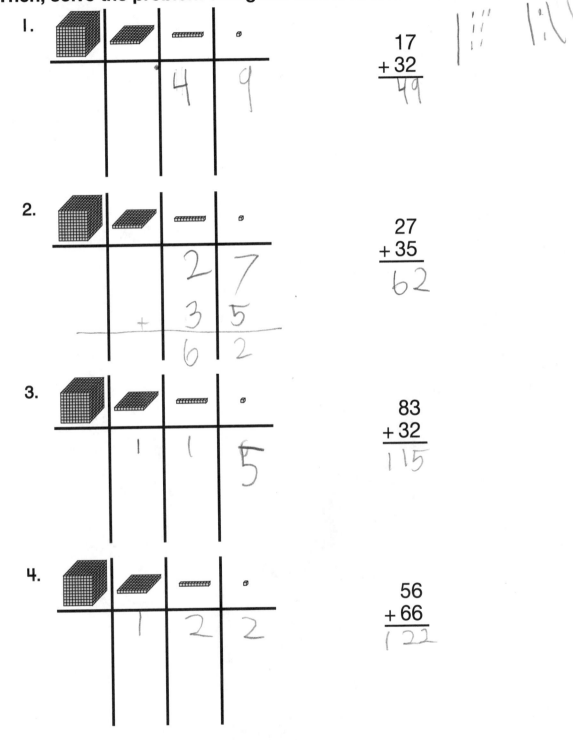

1.

$\begin{array}{r} 17 \\ + 32 \\ \hline 49 \end{array}$

2.

$\begin{array}{r} 27 \\ + 35 \\ \hline 62 \end{array}$

3.

$\begin{array}{r} 83 \\ + 32 \\ \hline 115 \end{array}$

4.

$\begin{array}{r} 56 \\ + 66 \\ \hline 122 \end{array}$

Solve the problems in two ways. You may use base-ten shorthand, Alda's shortcut method, or your own method.

5.   38
    + 42
    ———
      80

6.   77
    + 18
    ———
      95

7.   12
      35
    + 45
    ———
      92

8.   40
    + 82
    ———
     122

Clock

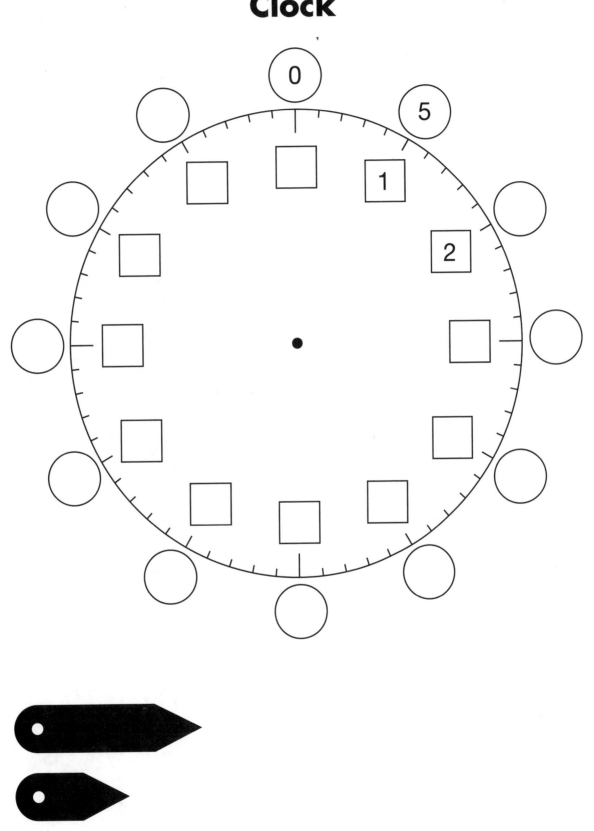

Area of Different Shapes

	Student Guide	Discovery Assignment Book	Adventure Book	Unit Resource Guide*
Lesson 1				
Measuring Area	●	●		
Lesson 2				
Boo the Blob		●		
Lesson 3				
The Better "Picker Upper"	●	●		
Lesson 4				
The Haunted House			●	
Lesson 5				
Joe the Goldfish				●
Lesson 6				
Using Number Sense at the Book Sale	●			

Unit Resource Guide pages are from the teacher materials.

Unit 5 Home Practice

PART 1

1. A. Half of 120 is _____   B. Half of 130 is _____

   C. Twice 80 is _____   D. Twice 95 is _____

2. For each of the problems below, write another number sentence that has the same difference.

   Example: 8 − 4 is the same as 10 − 6. We write 8 − 4 = 10 − 6.

   A. 14 − 7 = _____

   B. 17 − 8 = _____

   C. 12 − 5 = _____

PART 2

1. Natalie placed three skinnies and fifteen bits on her desk.

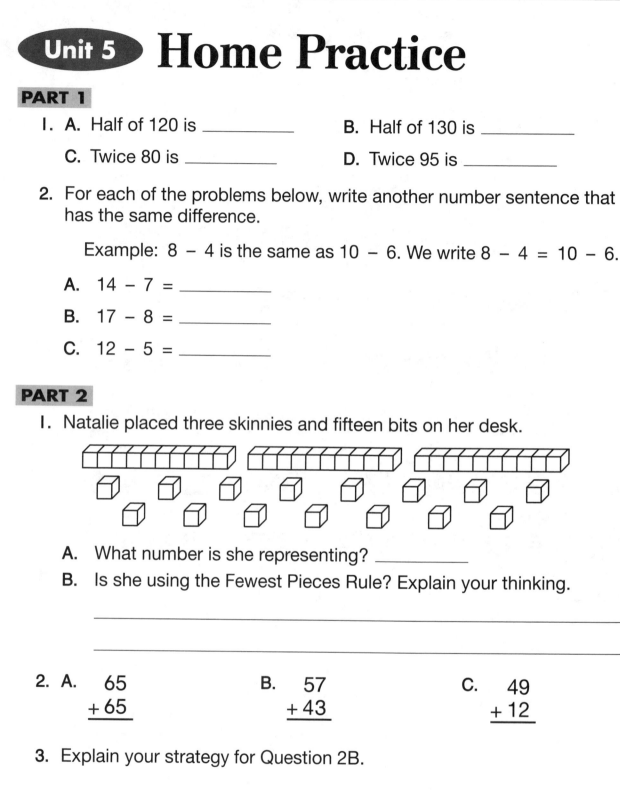

   A. What number is she representing? _____

   B. Is she using the Fewest Pieces Rule? Explain your thinking.

   _____

   _____

2. A. 65   B. 57   C. 49
      + 65   + 43   + 12

3. Explain your strategy for Question 2B.

AREA OF DIFFERENT SHAPES

Name _____ Date _____

PART 3

You will need *Centimeter Grid Paper* to complete Part 3.

1. Predict which shape has the greater area, Shape A or Shape B.

   _____

2. Find the area of each shape.

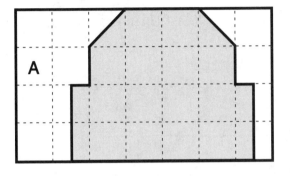

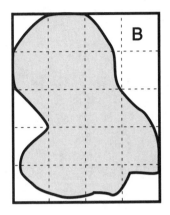

_____

_____

3. Corey measured the area of three spots of water. The areas of the three spots were 11 square centimeters, 8 square centimeters, and 6 square centimeters. Draw three spots on a sheet of *Centimeter Grid Paper* to show about how big these spots were.

PART 4

1. **A.** Draw a picture to illustrate Rami's story.

   Our coach took us to the batting cage. There were six of us. Six balls were pitched to each of us. It was a fun time!

   B. How many balls were pitched to Rami and his friends in all?

   _____

2. Hank bought three baseball key chains at the batting range, one for himself and one for each of his little brothers. One key chain costs 75¢. How much did Hank spend? Show how you solved the problem.

   _____

   _____

AREA OF DIFFERENT SHAPES   DAB • Grade 3 • Unit 5 **81**

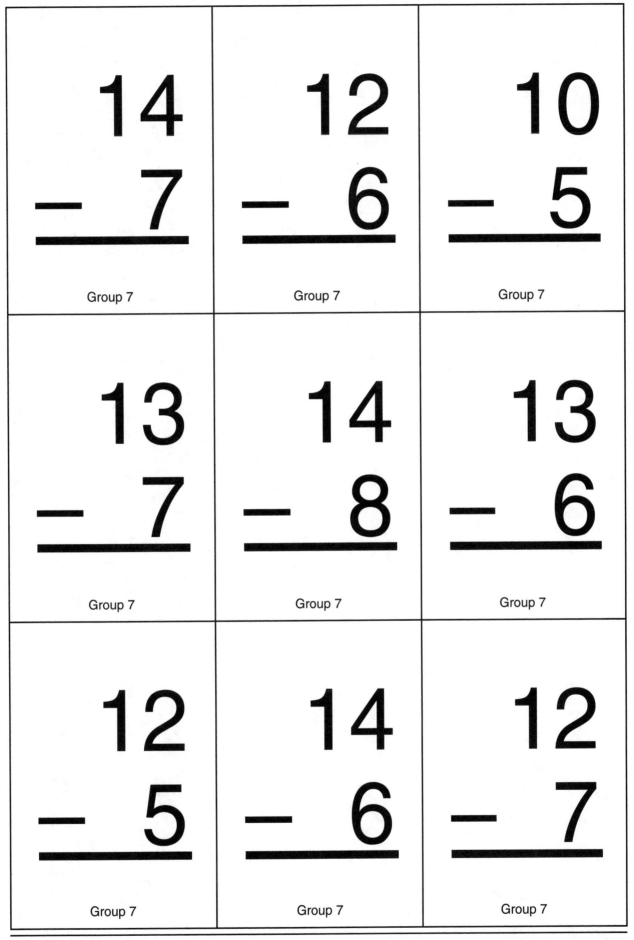

14	12	10
− 7	− 6	− 5
Group 7	Group 7	Group 7
13	14	13
− 7	− 8	− 6
Group 7	Group 7	Group 7
12	14	12
− 5	− 6	− 7
Group 7	Group 7	Group 7

AREA OF DIFFERENT SHAPES

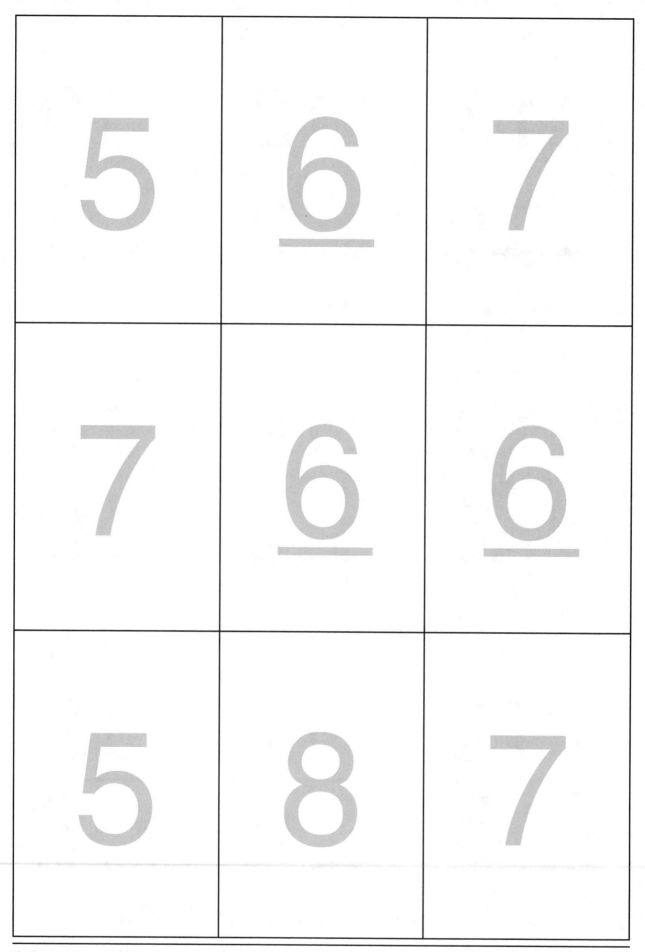

AREA OF DIFFERENT SHAPES

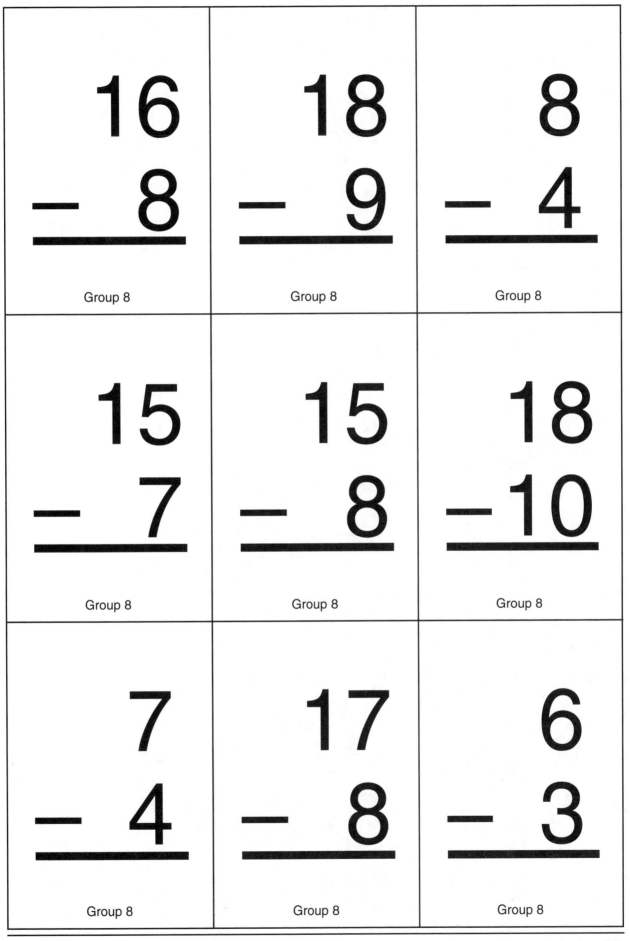

16 − 8	18 − 9	8 − 4
Group 8	Group 8	Group 8
15 − 7	15 − 8	18 −10
Group 8	Group 8	Group 8
7 − 4	17 − 8	6 − 3
Group 8	Group 8	Group 8

AREA OF DIFFERENT SHAPES

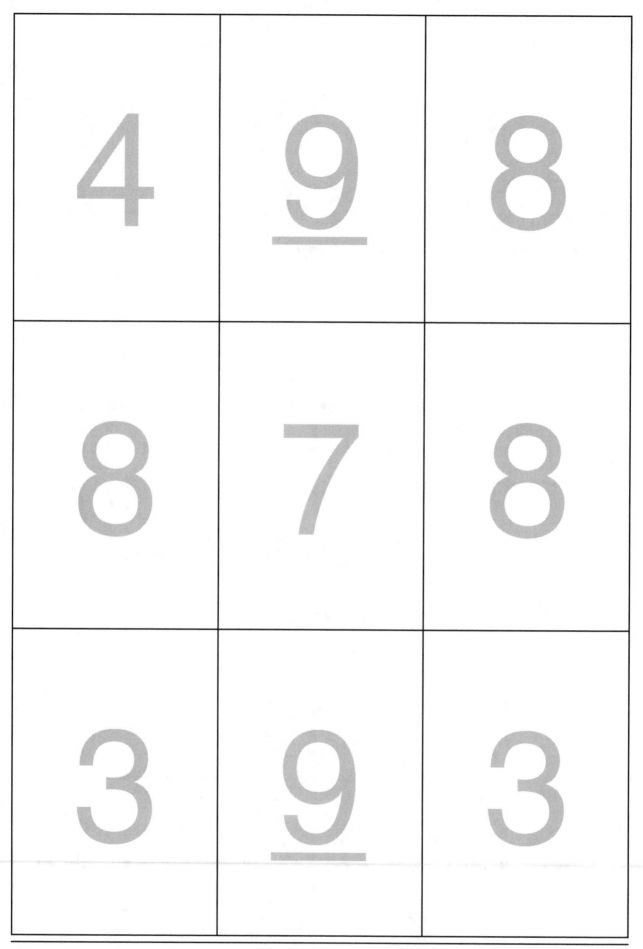

AREA OF DIFFERENT SHAPES

Area of Five Shapes

Homework

Find the area of each of the shapes on the grid below.

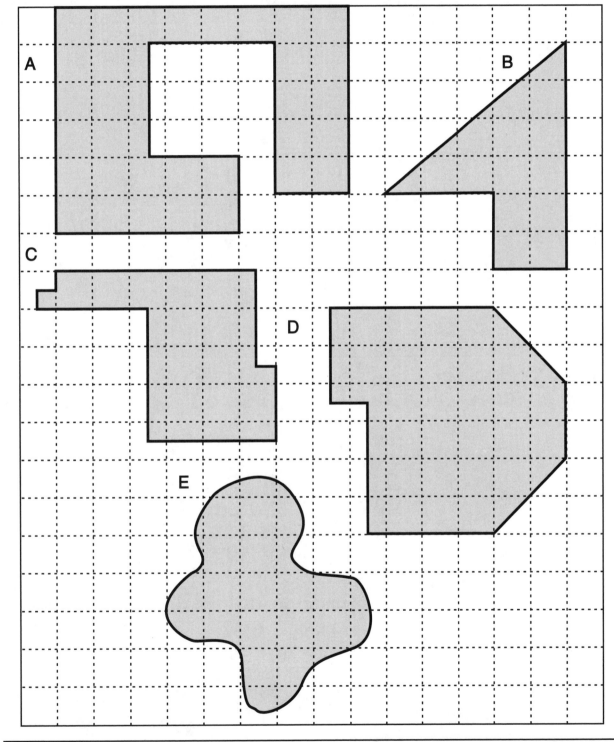

Name _____ Date _____

Boo the Blob Changes Shape

Boo the Blob is a very special creature who is completely flat. He tries to trick his friends by changing his shape. But his friends always know who he is because he cannot change his area.

Boo

One of the three blobs below is Boo in another form. Can you find him? Which one is he?

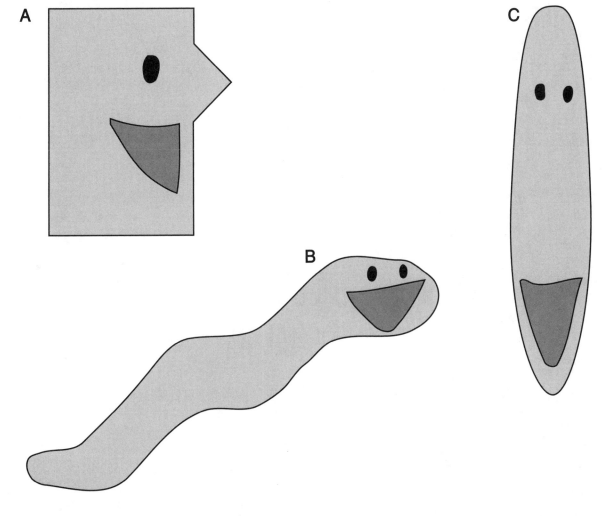

A

B

C

Record the area you counted for Shapes A, B, and C in the data table. Record and compare two classmates' data as well. Do not write anything in the column labeled "Median" yet.

Shape	Area in sq cm			
	My Data	**Classmate #1**	**Classmate #2**	**Median**
A				
B				
C				

1. List the three areas your group found for Shape A in order from smallest to largest. Circle the middle value.

   _____

2. The middle value is the **median.** Record the median area for Shape A in the data table.

3. Record the median values for Shapes B and C in the data table.

4. Which shape is Boo? Explain how your group decided.

   _____

   _____

   _____

   _____

The Better "Picker Upper"

Draw

Draw a picture of what you are going to do in the experiment. Label the variables in your picture.

1. What variables will you study in this experiment?

   _____

   _____

   _____

2. What variables should not change in this experiment? Explain.

   _____

   _____

3. What are you trying to find out in this experiment?

_____

_____

_____

4. Look carefully at each of your paper towels. Which towel do you think is the better "picker upper"? Explain.

_____

_____

_____

Collect

Work with your partners to do the experiment. Record your data in the table below. Don't forget to write the proper units for your measurements. How many drops of water will you use on each towel?

T Type of Towel	*A* Area of Spot (in _____) unit			
	Trial 1	**Trial 2**	**Trial 3**	**Median**

Graph your median data on a separate piece of graph paper.

Write your answers to the following questions.

5. Which towel had the spot with the largest area? What was the area of the spot?

_____

_____

6. Which towel had the spot with the smallest area?

_____

7. How much larger was the larger spot than the smallest spot? Explain how you found your answer.

_____

_____

_____

_____

8. How would the graph look if you dropped twice as many drops on each towel?

_____

_____

_____

_____

9. Choose one brand of paper towels. Predict how many drops of water it would take to cover one sheet *completely*. Explain how you made your prediction.

Brand of paper towel selected _____

Predicted number of drops to cover entire towel _____

_____

_____

_____

_____

_____

_____

10. Look at your data table and graph. Which towel do you think will soak up the most water? Why?

_____

_____

_____

_____

_____

_____

_____

Discuss

Discuss this question with your class.

11. If you could design another experiment with paper towels, what would it be? What variables would you choose to study? What variables should not change? Describe your experiment on a separate sheet of paper.

Lori's Questions

Lori did *The Better "Picker Upper"* using four different types of towels. She dropped two drops of water on each of the towels. Her graph is shown below.

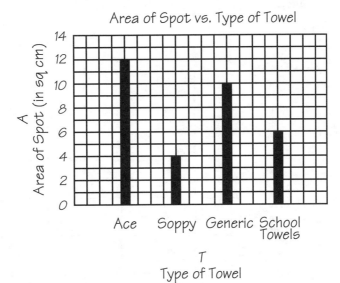

Area of Spot vs. Type of Towel

1. Which towel had a spot with an area of 10 sq cm? _____

2. Which towel will soak up the most water? Explain.

   _____

   _____

   _____

3. This is one of Lori's spots. She forgot to label it. Which towel is this spot from? Explain how you found out.

   _____

   _____

   _____

   _____

4. Lori did the experiment again, but this time she dropped five drops of water on a small paper towel. The picture on the right shows Lori's spot on her paper towel. How many drops of water do you think it would take to cover this towel completely? Carefully explain how you found your answer.

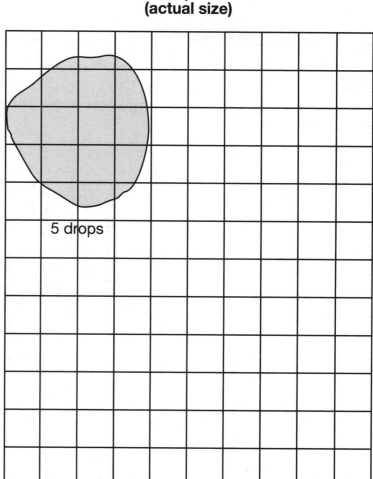

**Lori's Paper Towel
(actual size)**

5 drops

_____

_____

_____

_____

_____

_____

_____

_____

_____

Unit 6

More Adding and Subtracting

	Student Guide	Discovery Assignment Book	Adventure Book	Unit Resource Guide*
Lesson 1				
The 500 Hats				
Lesson 2				
The Coat of Many Bits	●			
Lesson 3				
Adding with Base-Ten Pieces	●	●		
Lesson 4				
Subtracting with Base-Ten Pieces	●	●		
Lesson 5				
Close Enough!	●			●
Lesson 6				
Leonardo the Blockhead			●	
Lesson 7				
Palindromes				
Lesson 8				
Digits Game		●		

Unit Resource Guide pages are from the teacher materials.

Unit 6 Home Practice

PART 1

1. A. 15 – 9 = _____   B. 17 – 10 = _____

   C. 9 – 4 = _____   D. 11 – 7 = _____

   E. 7 – 2 = _____   F. 12 – 3 = _____

   G. 14 – 8 = _____   H. 18 – 9 = _____

2. Leah has a hard time finding the answer to 1G. How did you find the answer to this subtraction fact? Share your method.

PART 2

1. Solve the addition and subtraction problems. Show how you solved each one.

   A. 156 + 54 = _____   B. 232 – 29 = _____

2. Sharon works at a flower shop. She received a shipment of roses and carnations. She received 48 roses. She received 60 more carnations than roses. Show how you solved the following problems.

   A. How many carnations did she receive? _____

   B. How many flowers did she receive in all? _____

PART 3

1. Mario covered a piece of paper with base-ten pieces. He used 4 flats and 16 skinnies. Beth said, "That's the same as 416 bits." Is Beth correct? Why or why not? Use base-ten shorthand to show your answer.

2. The middle school collected 1321 canned goods for a charity. The junior high school collected 1299 cans. The high school collected 2219 canned goods.

   A. Which school collected the most canned goods? _____

   B. Which school collected the least? _____

   C. List the numbers from largest to smallest. _____

   D. How many cans were collected in all? _____

PART 4

1. A. Ann Marie has some quarters, nickels, and dimes. She has ten coins in all. Half of them are quarters.

   What is the most money Ann Marie could have? _____
   Show how you solved this problem.

   B. What is the least amount Ann Marie could have? _____
   Show how you solved this problem.

2. At the zoo, Joe's dad bought 5 snow cones, one for each family member. One snow cone costs $1.26. How much do 5 snow cones cost? _____ Show how you found your answer.

Adding on the
Base-Ten Board

1. Nikia and Maruta both work at the TIMS Candy Company. Nikia
   made 136 Chocos. Maruta made 232 Chocos. How much candy did
   they make together? Solve the problem in two ways. Use base-ten
   shorthand and use numbers. Use base-ten pieces to help you.

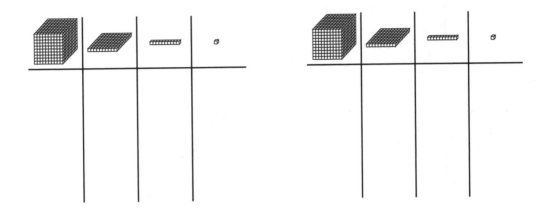

2. Another time Nikia made 237 Chocos and Maruta made 155. Find
   how much they made altogether. Solve the problem using base-ten
   shorthand and then with numbers. Make sure you use the Fewest
   Pieces Rule.

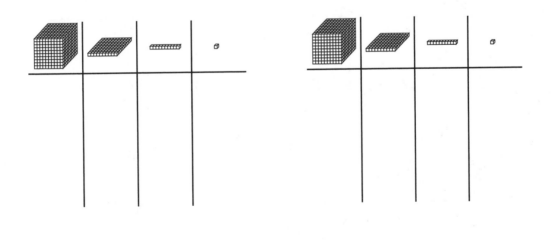

Do the following problems by drawing the base-ten pieces using base-ten shorthand. Then solve the problem using numbers. Use the Fewest Pieces Rule.

3. 69 + 23 + 18

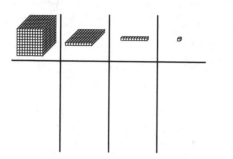   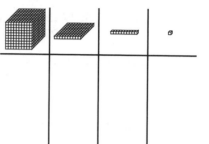

4. 324 + 194

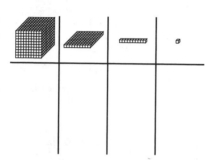   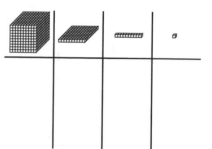

5. 607 + 148

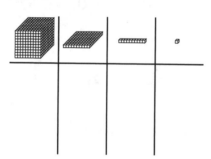   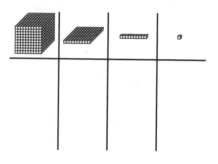

6. 1308 + 4196

Subtracting on the Base-Ten Board

Maruta and Nikia are helping out at the TIMS Candy Company Store. Many customers come in to buy Chocos. Maruta and Nikia need to keep track of how many Chocos are in the store. They use their *Base-Ten Boards* and *Recording Sheets* to keep track.

One day the store had 569 Chocos at the beginning of the day. During the day they sold 234 Chocos. How many were left?

Maruta put 5 flats, 6 skinnies, and 9 bits on the board. She then removed 4 bits, 3 skinnies, and 2 flats. There were 335 Chocos left.

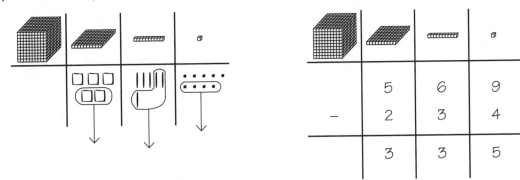

Another day Maruta and Nikia began with 423 Chocos. They sold 319 Chocos. How many were left?

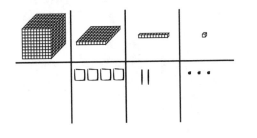

Maruta realized that she could not take 9 bits from 3 bits. She took a skinny and traded it for 10 bits.

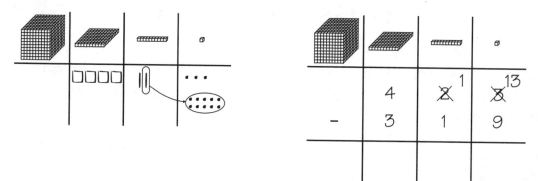

Then she had 13 skinnies and could take 9 away. She then took away the remaining skinny and 3 flats.

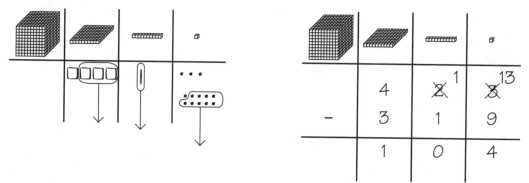

For each problem, help Maruta and Nikia compute how many Chocos they have left. Use base-ten pieces. Then use shorthand to sketch your work. Record your work in numbers on the second recording sheet.

I.

$$\begin{array}{r} 478 \\ -205 \\ \hline \end{array}$$

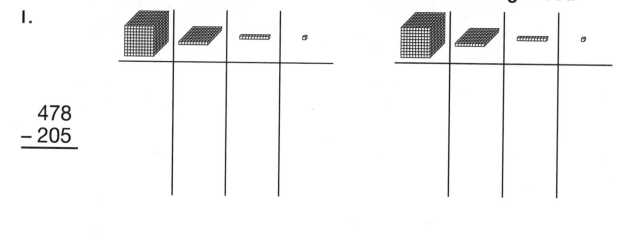

2.

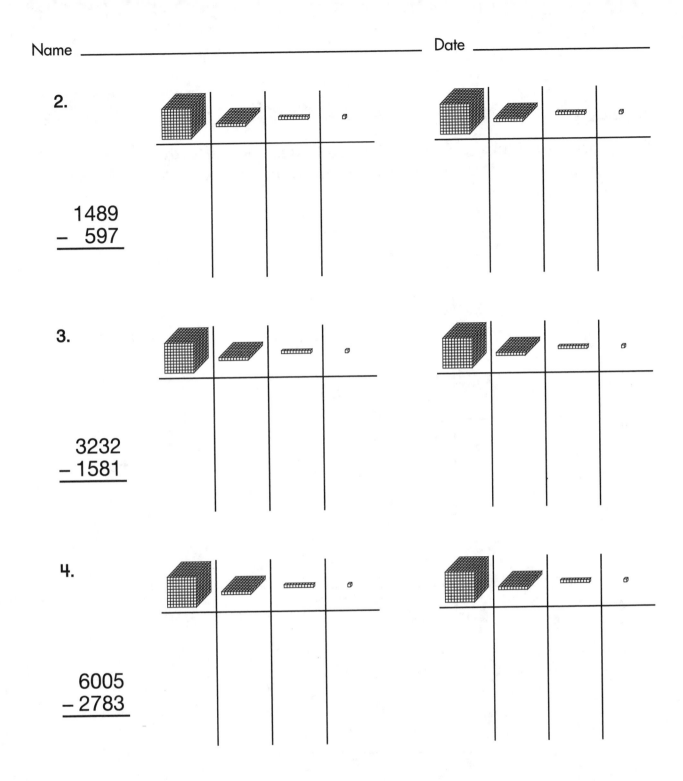

   1489
−   597

3.

   3232
− 1581

4.

   6005
− 2783

Name _____   Date _____

Solve each problem two ways. First, use base-ten shorthand on the recording sheet. Then use a shortcut method or mental math. Show or explain your method.

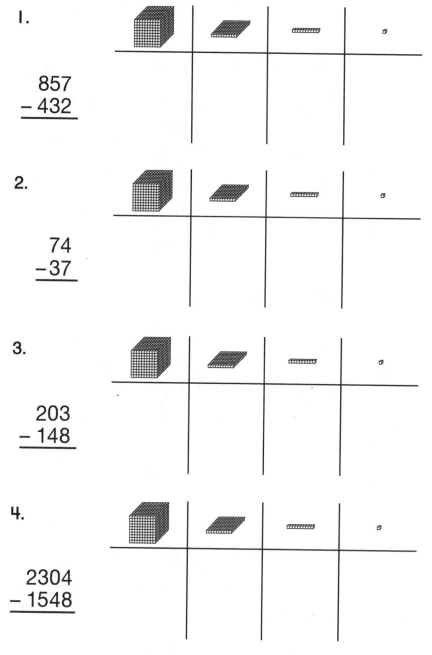

1.

857
− 432

2.

74
−37

3.

203
− 148

4.

2304
− 1548

Subtracting with Base-Ten Pieces

Digits Game

Players

This is a game for any number of players.

Materials

- one set of ten cards with the digits 0 through 9 written on them
- paper
- pencils

Rules

The object of the game is to get the largest answer to an addition or subtraction problem.

1. One person is the leader, and the others are players. The leader draws one playing board so that all of the players can see it. The playing board is a set of boxes arranged like an addition or subtraction problem. Here are some examples of playing boards:

   The leader draws only one playing board for each game.

2. Each player draws the playing board on his or her paper.

3. The leader tells the players to play for the largest answer. Then, he or she shuffles the cards, places them face down, picks the top card, and reads the digit to all the players.

4. Each player writes that digit in one of the boxes on his or her playing board. Each player must decide where to place the digit in order to get the largest answer. Once a player has written down a digit, it may not be moved. No digit will be repeated.

5. Placing the first card in a discard pile, the leader reads the next card from the top of the deck. Players place this digit in another unfilled box. Play continues until all the boxes are filled.

6. When all the boxes are filled, players add or subtract to find their answers, as indicated on the original playing board drawn by the leader. The player with the largest correct answer wins the game.

Another way to play the game is to have the smallest correct answer win the game.

Exploring Multiplication and Division

	Student Guide	Discovery Assignment Book	Adventure Book	Unit Resource Guide*
Lesson 1				
Lemonade Stand	●	●		
Lesson 2				
Katie's Job	●			●
Lesson 3				
Mathhoppers	●	●		
Lesson 4				
Birthday Party	●			
Lesson 5				
The Money Jar	●			●
Lesson 6				
Walking around Shapes		●		●

Unit Resource Guide pages are from the teacher materials.

Unit 7 Home Practice

PART 1

1. A. 12 + 8 + 5 = _____   2. A. 100 − 90 = _____

   B. 17 + 3 + 5 = _____   B. 110 − 90 = _____

   C. 5 + 16 + 4 = _____   C. 150 − 90 = _____

3. Sara said that she used the addition facts strategy "making a ten" to solve Questions 1A–1C. Explain how you could "make a ten" to solve each problem.

   _____

   _____

   _____

PART 2

1. A. 160 − 90 = _____   2. A. 160 + 40 = _____

   B. 160 − 100 = _____   B. 160 + 60 = _____

   C. 160 − 70 = _____   C. 160 + 80 = _____

3. Enrique and Derek bought ice cream. Together, they had $1.50. Derek bought a chocolate cone for $0.60 and Enrique bought a double-decker strawberry cone for $0.80.

   A. How much money will they have left after buying the ice cream cones? _____

   B. If they split the change evenly, how much money should each person get? _____

4. Erik wants to buy pencils at the school store. Each pencil costs 7 cents.

   How many pencils could he buy with 50 cents? _____
   Show how you solved the problem.

EXPLORING MULTIPLICATION AND DIVISION

PART 3

Use base-ten shorthand or a shortcut method to solve the following problems. Estimate to make sure your answers are reasonable.

1. 3496
    + 707

2. 4357
    + 2828

3. 359
    − 176

4. 3001
    − 1998

5. Explain your estimation strategy for Question 4.

_____

_____

_____

PART 4

1. Shelby has $5.00 in her piggy bank. Her piggy bank only has coins inside. What coins might Shelby have that add up to $5.00? Give at least two examples.

_____

_____

2. Jeffrey wants to visit his grandmother after his Little League game on Saturday. If his Little League game ends at 11:35 and it takes 25 minutes to travel to his grandmother's house, what time will Jeffrey begin his visit? _____ Show how you solved the problem.

Mr. Green's Giant Gumball Jamboree

Mr. Green sells giant gumballs for 20¢ each. Finish Mr. Green's data table of prices.

N Number of Gumballs	C Cents
1	
3	
5	
	140
9	

I. Explain how you figured out what to put in the data table. What patterns do you see in the data table?

_____

_____

_____

_____

2. Make a point graph of your data. Use the graph paper following Question 9.

   A. Finish numbering the axes.

   B. Label the axes.

   C. Title your graph.

3. Do the points form a pattern? If so, describe the pattern.

   _____

   _____

4. Can you use a ruler to draw a line through the points? Try it.

Solve Questions 5, 6, 7, and 8 in two ways. First, use your graph, showing your work with dotted lines. Then solve the problem another way to check your answer. (You can also solve the problem without the graph and use the graph to check.) Explain how you found your answers.

5. How much will 4 gumballs cost?

   _____

   _____

   _____

   _____

   _____

6. How many gumballs can you buy with $1.20? (Remember: $1.20 = 120¢)

   _____

   _____

   _____

   _____

   _____

7. How much will 10 gumballs cost?

_____

_____

_____

_____

_____

_____

_____

8. How many gumballs can you buy with $1.50?

_____

_____

_____

_____

_____

_____

_____

9. How much will 24 gumballs cost? Explain how you found your answer.

_____

_____

_____

_____

_____

_____

_____

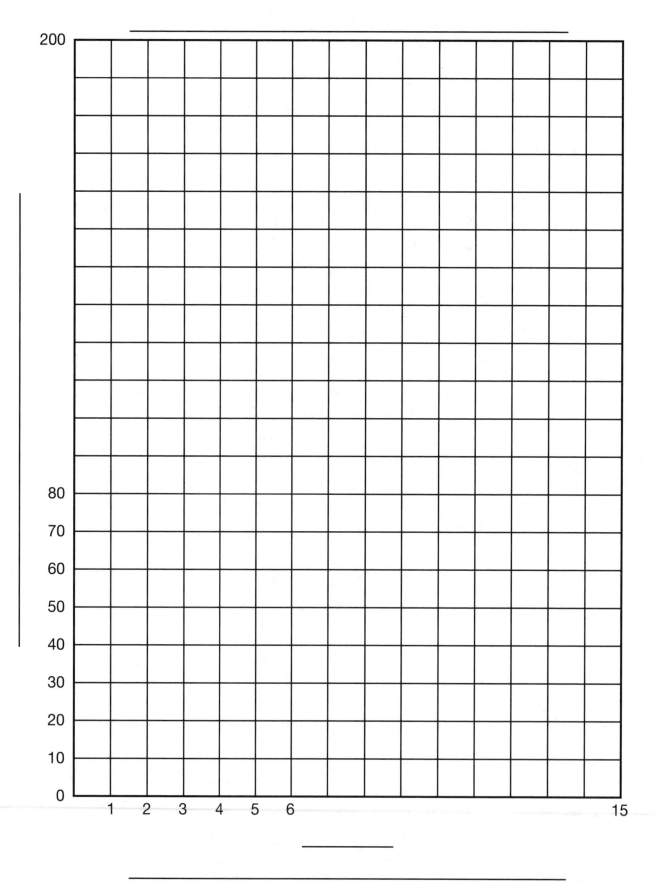

Name _____

Date _____

Mathhopper Number Line Template

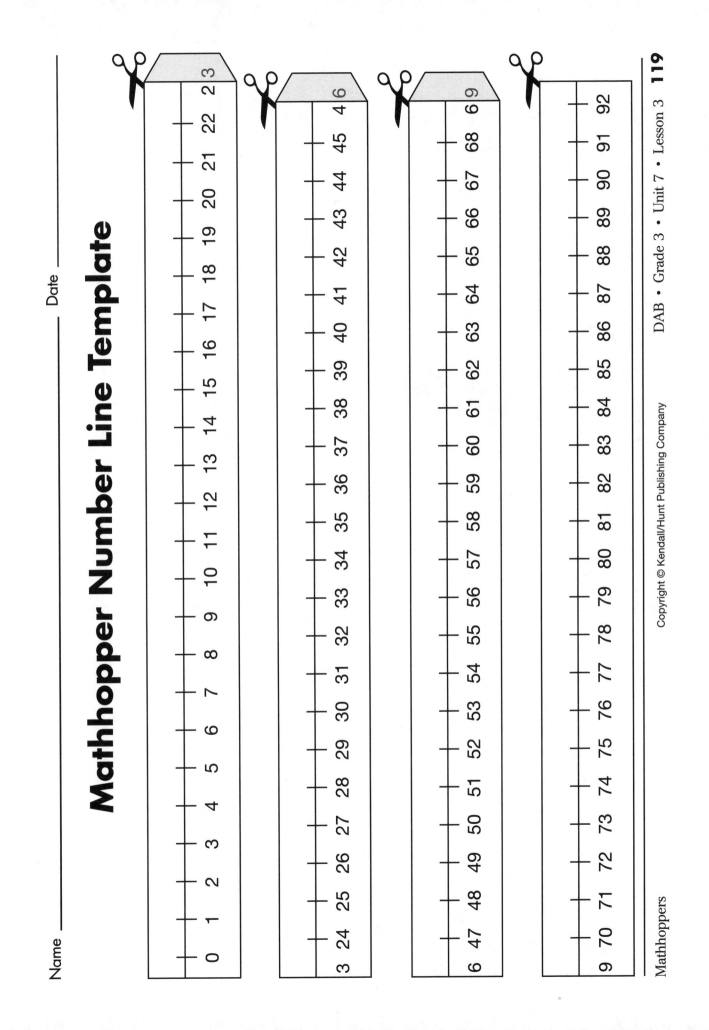

0 1 2 3 4 5 6 7 8 9 10 11 12 13 14 15 16 17 18 19 20 21 22 23

3 24 25 26 27 28 29 30 31 32 33 34 35 36 37 38 39 40 41 42 43 44 45 46

6 47 48 49 50 51 52 53 54 55 56 57 58 59 60 61 62 63 64 65 66 67 68 69

9 70 71 72 73 74 75 76 77 78 79 80 81 82 83 84 85 86 87 88 89 90 91 92

Professor Peabody's Mathhoppers

 **Homework**

Professor Peabody made up some mathhopper problems for his students. Since he's a bad typist, he missed some of the words. Sometimes he hit the wrong keys, erasing parts of the problems. Rewrite the problems for Professor Peabody, and fill in the blanks. He also needs you to give the solutions on another sheet of paper or on the back of this paper so he can check his students' work.

1. A +6 mathhopper started at 0 and hopped _____ times. On what number did it land?

2. A _____ mathhopper started at _____ and hopped _____ times. On what number did it land?

3. A mathhopper started at 0 and hopped _____ times until it reached _____. How big were its hops?

4. A _____.
   On what number did it land?

5. A _____.
   How many hops did it take?

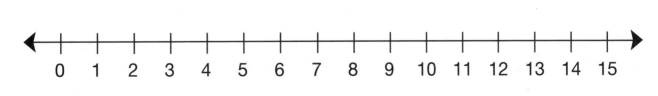

Walking around Shapes

When a bug walks all the way around the outside of a shape, the distance it walks is called the **perimeter.**

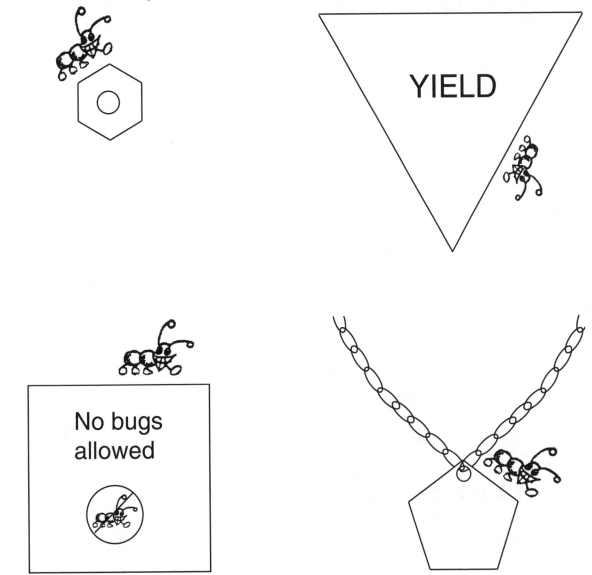

YIELD

No bugs
allowed

If all sides of a shape are the same length and all the angles are the same, we say the shape is a **regular** shape. Are all the shapes on this page regular shapes?

Walking around Triangles

For each triangle, measure the length of one side and the perimeter. Use the data table to record this information. Then fill in the last column. When you have finished, graph your data on a separate sheet of graph paper.

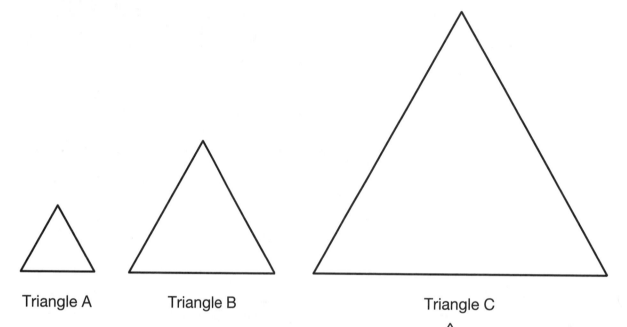

Triangle A   Triangle B   Triangle C

Shape: Equilateral Triangle

Triangle	L Length of a Side (in cm)	P Perimeter (in cm)	P ÷ L = ? Number Sentence
A			
B			
C			

Walking around Hexagons

For each hexagon, measure the length of one side and the perimeter. Use the data table to record this information. Then fill in the last column.

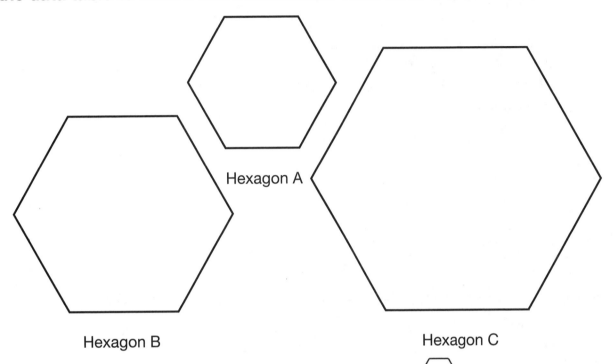

Hexagon A

Hexagon B

Hexagon C

Shape: Regular Hexagon

Hexagon	L _____ (in cm)	P _____ (in cm)	$P \div L = ?$ _____
A			
B			
C			

1. What patterns do you see in the hexagon data table?

   _____

   _____

   _____

2. Make a graph on a separate sheet of graph paper. Number the horizontal axis by ones; label this axis "Length of a Side." Number the vertical axis by twos; label this axis "Perimeter."

3. If the side of a regular hexagon is 6 centimeters, what is its perimeter? Explain how you found your answer.

   _____

   _____

   _____

   _____

4. Use a number sentence to solve Question 3 and show your work.

   _____

   _____

   _____

   _____

Walking around Squares

For each square, measure the length of one side and the perimeter. Use the data table to record this information. Then fill in the last column.

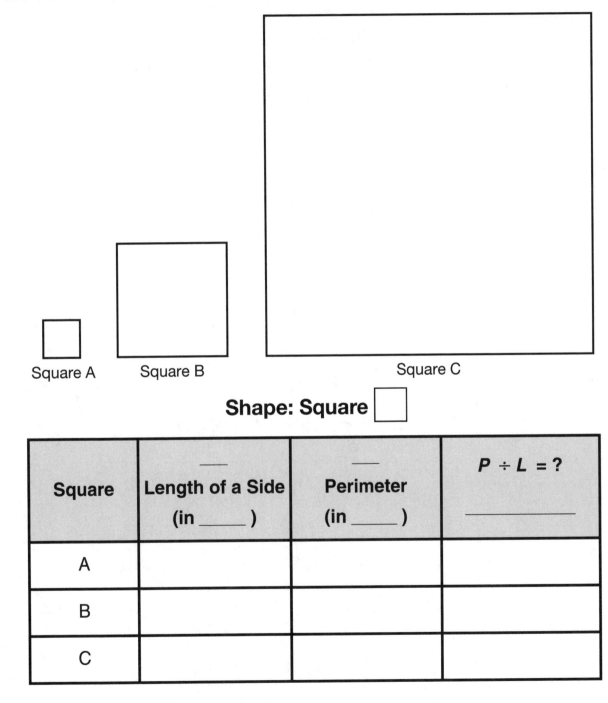

Square A   Square B   Square C

Shape: Square ⬜

Square	$\overline{}$ Length of a Side (in _____)	$\overline{}$ Perimeter (in _____)	$P \div L = ?$ $\overline{}$
A			
B			
C			

1. What patterns do you see in the square data table?

   _____

   _____

   _____

2. Make a graph on a separate sheet of graph paper. Number the horizontal axis by ones; label this axis "Length of a Side." Number the vertical axis by twos; label this axis "Perimeter."

3. What is the perimeter of a square that has a side 6 centimeters long? Explain how you found your answer, and draw the square.

   _____

   _____

Walking around Shapes

Unit 8

Mapping and Coordinates

	Student Guide	Discovery Assignment Book	Adventure Book	Unit Resource Guide*
Lesson 1				
Meet Mr. Origin	●			
Lesson 2				
Sara's Desk	●			●
Lesson 3				
Mapping a Tiny TIMS Town	●	●		●
Lesson 4				
The Ghost Galleons			●	
Lesson 5				
Tens Game	●			
Lesson 6				
Tall Buildings	●			

Unit Resource Guide pages are from the teacher materials.

⬭ Unit 8 Home Practice

1. **A.** 34 + 28 = _____   **B.** 42 − 39 = _____

2. **A.** 276 + 176 = _____   **B.** 35 − 18 = _____

3. **A.** 856 + 398 = _____   **B.** 519 − 378 = _____

4. Jillian had forty-six animal cards in her collection. Her mother gave her more cards for her birthday. Now Jillian has sixty-two cards in her collection. How many cards did her mother give her? Explain how you found your answer.

_____

_____

_____

PART 2

1. Mrs. Estrada is making costumes for her son's class play. She needs 10 buttons for each costume. Fill in the data in the table.

C Number of Costumes	B Number of Buttons
1	10
2	
3	

2. Mrs. Estrada needs 2 yards of material for each costume. Fill in the missing data in the table.

C Number of Costumes	B Number of Yards
1	
2	
3	

3. Buttons cost 10¢ each and material for the costume costs $5.00 a yard. If Mrs. Estrada has $35.00 to spend on the costumes, does she have enough to make 3 costumes? Show your work.

PART 3

1. A. 60 − 36 = _____   B. 28 + 17 + 13 = _____

2. A. 92 − 78 = _____   B. 35 + 25 + 19 = _____

3. A. 180 − 90 = _____   B. 46 + 38 + 54 = _____

4. Billy makes 95 cents a week helping his grandmother. How much will he make in 3 weeks? Explain how you found your answer.

_____

_____

_____

PART 4

You need $\frac{1}{2}$ cup of butter to make 10 cookies.

Complete the data table. Use the data to make a point graph.

B Cups of Butter	C Number of Cookies
$\frac{1}{2}$ c	
1 c	
2 c	

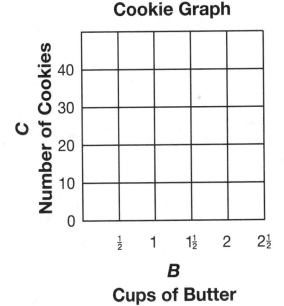

Cookie Graph

How much butter will it take to make 30 cookies? Explain how you found your answer.

_____

_____

_____

Tiny TIMS Town Data Tables

Building	Right (in _____)	Front (in _____)
library		
market		
bank		
school		

Building	Distance Using the Map (in _____)	Distance in TIMS Town (in _____)	Error (in _____)
bank to market			
market to school			
library to nearest building			

Unit 9

Using Patterns to Predict

	Student Guide	Discovery Assignment Book	Adventure Book	Unit Resource Guide*
Lesson 1				
Measuring Mass	●			●
Lesson 2				
Mass vs. Number	●	●		●
Lesson 3				
More Mass Problems	●			

Unit Resource Guide pages are from the teacher materials.

Unit 9 Home Practice

PART 1

1. A. 18 + 15 + 3 = _____   B. 500 − 300 = _____

2. A. 80 − 50 = _____   B. 50 + 40 + 9 = _____

3. Lindy bought an airmail stamp for 60¢. She gave the clerk one dollar.

    A. How much change should she get back? _____

    B. What coins might the clerk give her? _____

    _____

    C. Give another combination of coins the clerk might give Lindy.

    _____

4. Solve the problems. Estimate to be sure your answers are reasonable and explain your strategies.

    A.   7943
        + 158

    B.   2000
        − 874

PART 2

1. A ball balances nine 10-gram masses and three 5-gram masses.

    What is the mass of the ball? _____

2. A marker balances three 10-gram masses, nine 5-gram masses, and three 1-gram masses. What is the mass of the marker?

    _____

3. A box that has 3 crayons in it has a total mass of 60 grams. What is

    the mass of one crayon? _____

PART 3

Give the location of each shape for this map.

Front

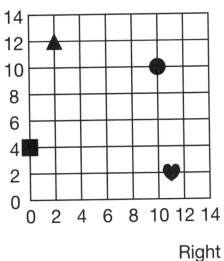

Shape	Right	Front
▲		
■		
●		
♥		

Right

PART 4

Find the area of the shapes on both the grid and the geoboard.

This is one sq cm.

One square unit

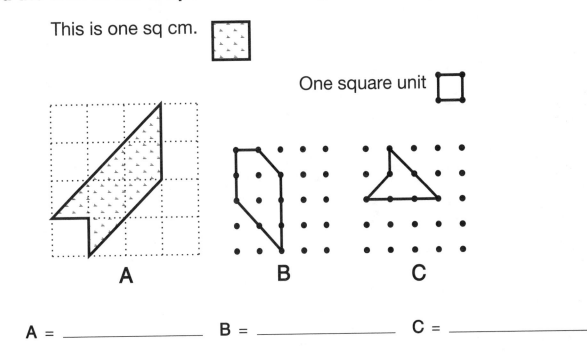

A   B   C

A = _____   B = _____   C = _____

Investigating Mass vs. Number

Draw a picture of what you are going to do in this experiment. Label the variables in your picture.

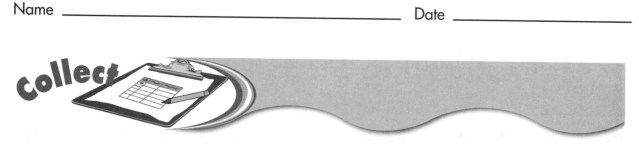

Get seven or more objects that look the same. Use a data table like the one below. But before you begin, discuss with your class the values of *N* you will put in the table. Make your measurements and record your data in a table like the one below.

N Number of _____	M Mass (in _____) unit

Graph your data on a piece of graph paper. Will you make a bar graph or a point graph?

Discuss with your class which variable you will graph on the horizontal axis and which variable you will graph on the vertical axis. Then discuss with your group how to number the axes. You will probably have to skip count on at least one of the axes. Be sure to start numbering with zero.

Explore

Use your data to help you answer the following questions.

1. What patterns do you see in your data points? Which of the following

   looks most like your graph? _____

   A   B   C

2. Draw a **best-fit line** for your data points.

3. **A.** Predict the mass of five of your objects using the pattern in your

      graph. _____

   B. Check your prediction by measuring the mass of five of your

      objects. What is the actual mass? _____

   C. Was your prediction close? _____
      Explain why you think this.

      _____

      _____

      _____

4. Find another way to predict the mass of five objects. (Do not use your
   graph.) Show your work. Is this new prediction better, worse, or about

   the same? _____

5. **A.** Predict the mass of seven of your objects. Write down your
prediction, and explain how you made it. _____

_____

_____

B. Check your prediction by massing seven of your objects. What is
the actual mass? _____

Was your prediction close? _____

Explain why you think this.

_____

_____

6. Use your graph to predict the mass of $5\frac{1}{2}$ of your objects. How did
you get your answer?   _____

_____

_____

_____

_____

7. **A.** Predict about how many of your objects you will need to get a
total mass of 100 g. Write down your prediction. _____

B. Check your prediction. Explain how you checked your prediction.

_____

_____

_____

Unit 10

Numbers and Patterns: An Assessment Unit

	Student Guide	Discovery Assignment Book	Adventure Book	Unit Resource Guide*
Lesson 1				
Stencilrama	●	●		
Lesson 2				
Problem Game	●	●		
Lesson 3				
Class Party				●
Lesson 4				
Word Problems for Review	●			
Lesson 5				
Midyear Test				●

Unit Resource Guide pages are from the teacher materials.

Unit 10 Home Practice

PART 1

Do these problems in your head. Write only the answers.

1. 16 − 8 = _____
2. 17 − 8 = _____
3. 170 − 80 = _____
4. 18 − 9 = _____
5. 18 − 10 = _____
6. 150 − 70 = _____
7. 14 − 7 = _____
8. 14 − 8 = _____
9. 120 − 70 = _____
10. 14 − 6 = _____
11. 12 − 5 = _____
12. 120 − 50 = _____

13. 100
    − 50

14.   80
    − 40

15. 150
    − 80

PART 2

Put a digit (1, 2, 3, 4, 5, 6, 7, 8, 9, or 0) in each box. Use each digit once or not at all. Subtract to find your answers.

☐☐☐☐ − ☐☐☐☐ =

1. What is the biggest answer you can get? _____

2. What is the smallest answer you can get? _____

3. If a digit can be used more than once, then what is the biggest answer you can get? _____

4. If a digit can be used more than once, then what is the smallest answer you can get? _____

Solve the following problems. Estimate to be sure your answers are reasonable.

5.   1234
   − 567

6.   912
   − 569

7.   807
   − 696

8. Show your estimation strategy for Question 5.

PART 3

1. Suppose we use the following standard masses to measure mass using a balance: 8-gram masses, 4-gram masses, and 1-gram masses. Think about how many of each you would need to use to balance a bottle of glue with a mass of 54 grams.

   A. How many of each would you need if you used the smallest number of masses possible?

   _____

   B. How many of each would you need if you used the largest number of masses possible?

   _____

2. Using the same standard masses, think about how many of each you would need to balance a note pad with a mass of 58 grams.

   A. How many of each would you need if you used the smallest number of masses possible?

   _____

   B. If you started with eight 4-gram masses, how many 8-gram and 1-gram masses would you still need to balance the note pad?

   _____

PART 4

1. Mr. Sosa teaches art class from 8:00 A.M. until 3:30 P.M. every Saturday. How many hours does he work on one Saturday?

   _____

2. How many hours will Mr. Sosa have worked after 4 Saturdays?

   _____

3. Last Saturday Mr. Sosa started art class at 8:00 A.M. He got sick and ended class $3\frac{1}{2}$ hours later. What time did he end the class?

   _____

Stencilrama

1. What variables are you going to compare in this experiment?

   _____

   _____

2. What variables should not change in this experiment?

   _____

   _____

Draw a picture of what you are going to do in this experiment. Label the variables.

Work with your partner to collect the data which will help you solve problems about the length of a border and the number of times you used your stencil.

N Number of Stencils	L Length of Border (in inches)

Make a point graph of your data on a sheet of graph paper. You will need to use your graph to solve problems about length and the number of times you used your stencil.

Explore

3. **A.** Measure the length of three stencils. _____

   B. Check your graph. Use the graph to find the length of three stencils. **Show how you used your graph to find the length.** (You will need to mark on your graph.)

   C. Length of three stencils from graph: _____

   Are your answers the same? Why or why not?

4. **A.** Use your graph to predict the length of seven stencils. **Show your work on the graph.** (You will need to mark on your graph.)

   Predicted length of seven stencils: _____

   B. Find the length of seven stencils another way. Describe how you found your answer.

5. **A.** Use your graph to predict the number of times you will need to use your stencil to make a border the length of your long sheet of paper. **Show your work on the graph.**

   Predicted number of stencils: _____

B. Solve the problem another way to check. Tell how you solved the problem.

6. **A.** Find the number of times you will need to use your stencil to

make a border across the _____.

(Write the name of something you could decorate with a border in the blank. Your teacher will help you choose.)

B. Describe how you solved the problem.

Problem Game Board

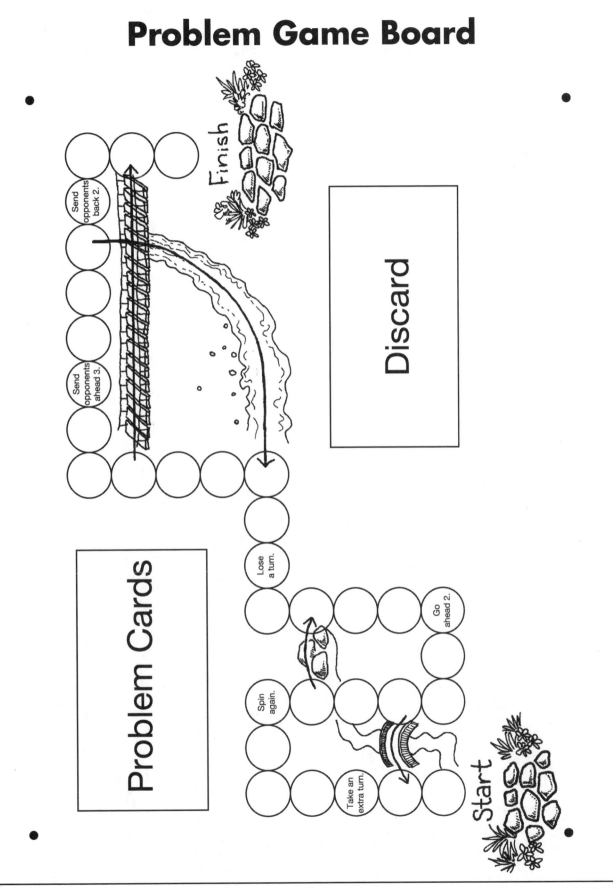

Problem Game Spinner

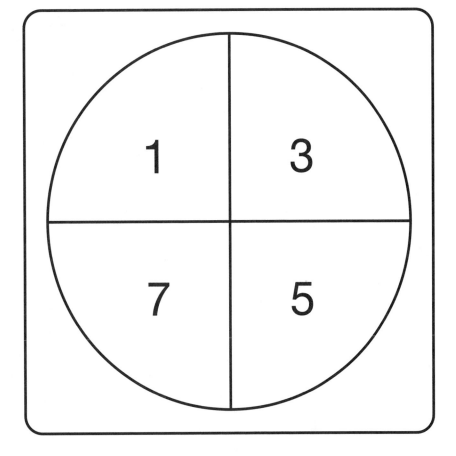

Unit 11

Multiplication Patterns

	Student Guide	Discovery Assignment Book	Adventure Book	Unit Resource Guide*
Lesson 1				
Lizardland Problems	●			
Lesson 2				
Handy Facts		●		
Lesson 3				
Multiplication and Rectangles	●			
Lesson 4				
Completing the Table	●	●		
Lesson 5				
Floor Tiler		●		
Lesson 6				
Division in Lizardland	●			
Lesson 7				
Cipher Force!			●	
Lesson 8				
Multiples of Tens and Hundreds	●	●		

*Unit Resource Guide pages are from the teacher materials.

155

Unit 11 Home Practice

PART 1

1. 160 – 70 = _____   2. 120 – 50 = _____   3. 140 – 60 = _____

4. 82 + _____ = 100   5. 53 + _____ = 100   6. 44 + _____ = 100

7. When Tony cleaned his mom's car he found some coins under the seats. His mom let him keep the coins and gave him $.25 more for cleaning the car. Now he has $2.00.

   A. How much money did Tony find in the car? _____

   B. What coins and how many of each could he have found?
       Give two possible answers.

PART 2

1. 600 + 700 = _____   2. 400 + 800 = _____   3. 500 + 900 = _____

4. 1000 – _____ = 450   5. 1000 – _____ = 343

6. Tina's high school graduating class has 321 students. Rita's junior high graduating class has 132 students. Sara, who is graduating from kindergarten, is in a class of 42 students.

   A. How many more students are in Tina's class than in Rita's?

   B. If all three classes attend the same ceremony, how many students would be graduating?

PART 3

1. On a piece of graph paper, draw as many rectangles as you can with an area of 18 square centimeters. Write a number sentence inside each rectangle to find the area of that rectangle.

2. A +6 mathhopper takes 8 hops. Where will it land? _____

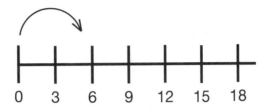

3. What is the approximate area of Olga the Oval? _____

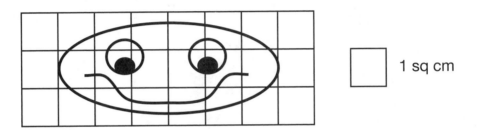

1 sq cm

PART 4

1. How many leaves do 9 four-leaf clovers have? _____

2. Write a story and draw a picture about 6×3. Write a number sentence for your picture.

3. **A.** Describe a triangle in as few words as possible. _____

   _____

   _____

   B. Make a list of some triangles in your home. _____

   _____

My Multiplication Table

Fill in the columns that are starred.

☆ ☆ ☆ ☆   ☆   ☆

×	0	1	2	3	4	5	6	7	8	9	10
0	0										
1											
2											
3											
4											
5											
6											
7											
8											
9											
10											

In your journal, write about the patterns you see in the table. Try to find a pattern for each starred column.

Save this table. You will fill in more facts later.

Practicing Handy Facts

Solve the following problems. Use your multiplication table when you need help.

1. $3 \times 2 = $ _____
2. $6 \times 10 = $ _____
3. $0 \times 10 = $ _____
4. $6 \times 5 = $ _____
5. $8 \times 10 = $ _____
6. $7 \times 1 = $ _____
7. $4 \times 1 = $ _____
8. $9 \times 3 = $ _____
9. $6 \times 2 = $ _____
10. $1 \times 4 = $ _____
11. $9 \times 5 = $ _____
12. $5 \times 5 = $ _____

13.
$$\begin{array}{r} 7 \\ \times\,5 \\ \hline \end{array}$$

14.
$$\begin{array}{r} 7 \\ \times\,2 \\ \hline \end{array}$$

15.
$$\begin{array}{r} 8 \\ \times\,5 \\ \hline \end{array}$$

16.
$$\begin{array}{r} 3 \\ \times\,3 \\ \hline \end{array}$$

17.
$$\begin{array}{r} 3 \\ \times\,5 \\ \hline \end{array}$$

18.
$$\begin{array}{r} 6 \\ \times\,0 \\ \hline \end{array}$$

19.
$$\begin{array}{r} 0 \\ \times\,2 \\ \hline \end{array}$$

20.
$$\begin{array}{r} 1 \\ \times\,3 \\ \hline \end{array}$$

21.
$$\begin{array}{r} 4 \\ \times\,5 \\ \hline \end{array}$$

22.
$$\begin{array}{r} 2 \\ \times\,3 \\ \hline \end{array}$$

23.
$$\begin{array}{r} 2 \\ \times\,5 \\ \hline \end{array}$$

24.
$$\begin{array}{r} 5 \\ \times\,2 \\ \hline \end{array}$$

Write and solve a multiplication story about zero. Write a number sentence to go with it.

_____

_____

_____

_____

_____

Nickels and Dimes

Homework

1. Complete the following table by counting money (real or pretend) or by using arithmetic.

Number of Nickels	Number of Dimes	Value of Nickels	Value of Dimes	Total Value
5	3	$.25	$.30	$.55
7	2			
	4	$.40		
	8	$.30		
2			$.90	
4			$1.00	
3			$.30	$.45
		$.05	$.50	
0	7			
9			$.10	$.55

2. How many ways can you make $.45 using only nickels and dimes? List them in the table below.

Number of Nickels	Number of Dimes	Value of Nickels	Value of Dimes	Total Value

Handy Facts

Triangle Flash Cards: 5s

- Work with a partner. Each partner cuts out the flash cards below.
- Your partner chooses one card at a time and covers the shaded corner.
- Multiply the two uncovered numbers.
- Divide the cards into three piles: those facts you know and can answer quickly, those you can figure out with a strategy, and those you need to learn.
- Practice the last two piles again. Then make a list of the facts you need to practice at home.
- Repeat the directions for your partner.

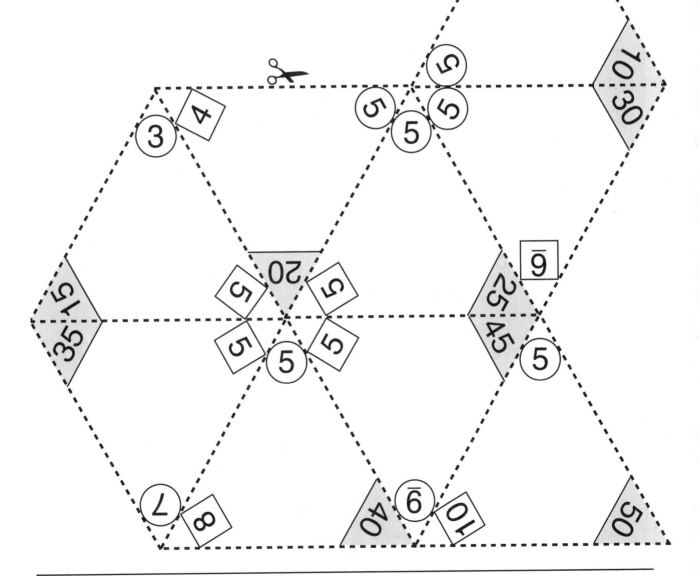

Triangle Flash Cards: 10s

- Work with a partner. Each partner cuts out the flash cards below.
- Your partner chooses one card at a time and covers the shaded corner.
- Multiply the two uncovered numbers.
- Divide the cards into three piles: those facts you know and can answer quickly, those you can figure out with a strategy, and those you need to learn.
- Practice the last two piles again. Then make a list of the facts you need to practice at home.
- Repeat the directions for your partner.

Completing the Table

Multiplication Facts I Know

- **Circle the facts you know well.**
- **Keep this table and use it to help you multiply.**
- **As you learn more facts, you may circle them too.**

×	0	1	2	3	4	5	6	7	8	9	10
0	0	0	0	0	0	0	0	0	0	0	0
1	0	1	2	3	4	5	6	7	8	9	10
2	0	2	4	6	8	10	12	14	16	18	20
3	0	3	6	9	12	15	18	21	24	27	30
4	0	4	8	12	16	20	24	28	32	36	40
5	0	5	10	15	20	25	30	35	40	45	50
6	0	6	12	18	24	30	36	42	48	54	60
7	0	7	14	21	28	35	42	49	56	63	70
8	0	8	16	24	32	40	48	56	64	72	80
9	0	9	18	27	36	45	54	63	72	81	90
10	0	10	20	30	40	50	60	70	80	90	100

Floor Tiler

Players

This is a game for two to four players.

Materials

- $\frac{1}{2}$ sheet of *Centimeter Grid Paper* per player
- *Spinner 1–4*
- *Spinner 1–10*
- a crayon or marker for each player

Rules

1. The first player makes two spins so that he or she has two numbers. The player may either spin one spinner twice or spin each spinner once.

2. The player must then find the **product** of the two numbers he or she spun. For example, $3 \times 4 = $ **12**.

3. After finding the product, the player colors in a rectangle that has the same number of grid squares on the grid paper. For example, he or she might color in 3 rows of 4 squares for a total of 12 squares. But the player could have colored in 2 rows of 6 squares or 1 row of 12 squares instead. (Remember, the squares colored in must connect so that they form a rectangle.)

4. Once the player has made his or her rectangle, the player draws an outline around it and writes its number sentence inside. For example, a player who colored in 3 rows of 4 squares would write "$3 \times 4 = 12$." A player who colored in 2 rows of 6 squares would write "$2 \times 6 = 12$."

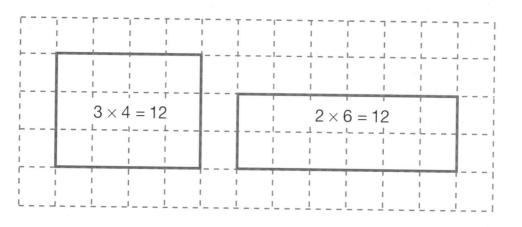

5. Players take turns spinning and filling in their grids.

6. If a player is unable to fill in a rectangle for his or her spin, he or she loses the turn, and the next player can play.

7. The first player to fill in his or her grid paper completely wins the game.

8. If no player is able to color in a rectangle in three rounds of spinning, the player with the fewest squares of the grid left is the winner.

Spinners 1–4 and 1–10

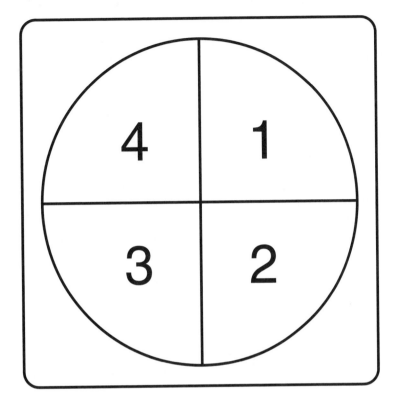

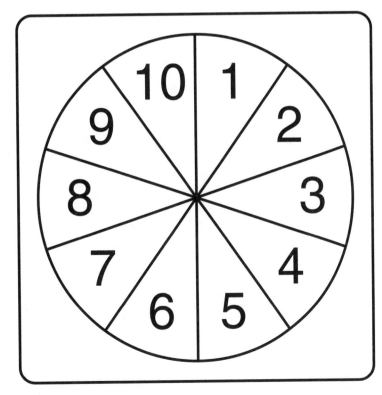

Professor Peabody's Multiplication Tables

Homework

Professor Peabody started to fill in the multiplication table below. He wanted to look for patterns. As he was working, a rare spotted mathhopper hopped by his window. He quickly picked up his net and followed it out the window.

Help Professor Peabody with his work by finishing this table for him. Look for patterns. On a separate sheet of paper, write a report that tells Professor Peabody about the patterns you find.

X	10	20	30	40	50	60	70	80	90	100
1									90	100
2			60					160	180	
3							210	240		
4						240	280			
5					250	300				500
6				240	300					
7			210	280						
8		160	240						720	
9	90	180								
10	100									

Unit 12

Dissections

	Student Guide	Discovery Assignment Book	Adventure Book	Unit Resource Guide*
Lesson 1				
Tangrams	●	●		●
Lesson 2				
Building with Triangles	●	●		●
Lesson 3				
Building with Four Triangles	●			●
Lesson 4				
Dissection Puzzles	●	●		
Lesson 5				
Hex		●		
Lesson 6				
Focus on Word Problems	●			

Unit Resource Guide pages are from the teacher materials.

Unit 12 Home Practice

PART 1

Estimate to be sure your answers are reasonable.

1. 285
   +300

2. 285
   +318

3. 872
   −400

4. 872
   −490

5. Explain your estimation strategy for Question 4.

6. Marie has 748 marbles in her collection. She wants 1000. How many more marbles does she need?

PART 2

1. 115
   +27

2. 127
   +74

3. 280
   −33

4. 325
   −76

5. Explain a strategy for using mental math for Question 3.

6. Ted read a book for 43 minutes on Saturday and 29 minutes on Sunday.
   A. Did Ted read for more than one hour? Explain how you know.

   B. How many minutes did Ted read? _____

PART 3

Girl Scout Troop 903 went to Lizardland. Thirty-five girls were accompanied by seven adults. Use this information to solve the following problems:

1. The Girl Scout troop is standing in line for the Leaping Lizard roller coaster. There are 8 cars on the roller coaster and each car can hold 4 people. Can the entire group ride the roller coaster at one time? Explain.

2. If 8 people can ride the Lizard-Go-Round at the same time, how many rides will it take for all the girls to ride one time? Explain.

3. The troop is standing in line for the Bump-a-Lizard bumper cars. Each car holds 2 people. How many bumper cars will the troop need for everyone in the group? Explain.

4. The Curly-Whirly-Lizard ride fits 3 people per car. There are 15 cars on the ride.

    A.   Can the entire group ride the ride at the same time? Explain.

    B.   If one adult rode in a car of girls, how many cars would not have an adult?

PART 4

1. Look at the six shapes below. Draw an **X** on the right angle(s) inside the shapes.

2. If any of the six shapes are symmetrical, draw in the lines of symmetry that divide the shape in half.

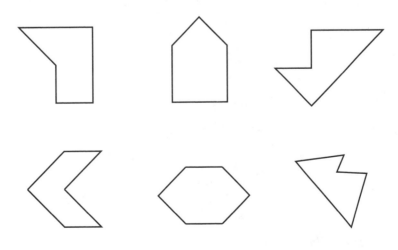

Triangle Flash Cards: 2s

- Work with a partner. Each partner cuts out the flash cards below.
- Your partner chooses one card at a time and covers the shaded corner.
- Multiply the two uncovered numbers.
- Divide the cards into three piles: those facts you know and can answer quickly, those you can figure out with a strategy, and those you need to learn.
- Practice the last two piles again. Then make a list of the facts you need to practice at home.
- Repeat the directions for your partner.

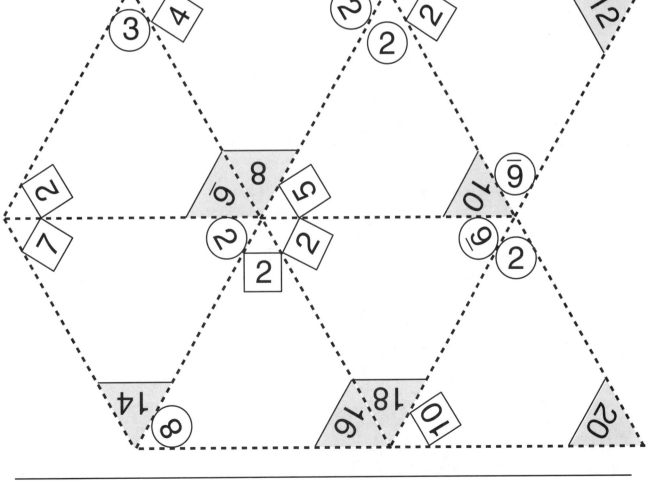

Triangle Flash Cards: 3s

- Work with a partner. Each partner cuts out the flash cards below.
- Your partner chooses one card at a time and covers the shaded corner.
- Multiply the two uncovered numbers.
- Divide the cards into three piles: those facts you know and can answer quickly, those you can figure out with a strategy, and those you need to learn.
- Practice the last two piles again. Then make a list of the facts you need to practice at home.
- Repeat the directions for your partner.

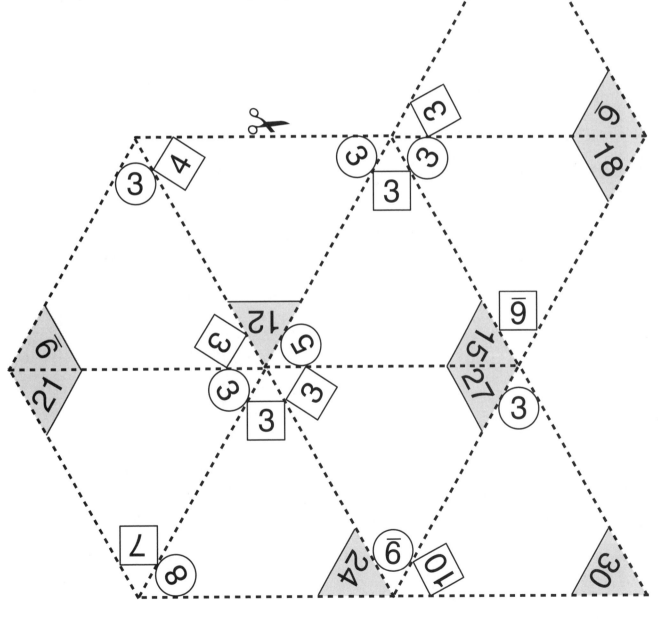

Making a Tangram Puzzle

Make up your own tangram puzzle.

- Create a design using all seven tangram pieces.
- Make sure your pieces touch without overlapping.
- Then make an outline of your design in the space below.
- Trade tangrams with a friend. Try to solve each other's tangrams.

Building with Triangles
Data Table 1

Number of triangles used _____ Partner(s) _____

Name of Shape	Sketch	No. of Sides	No. of Corners (vertices)	No. of Right Angles	Area (sq in)	Perimeter (cm)

Name _____ Date _____

Building with Triangles
Data Table 2

Number of triangles used _____ Partner(s) _____

Name of Shape	Sketch	No. of Sides	No. of Corners (vertices)	No. of Right Angles	Area (sq in)	Perimeter (cm)

Puzzle Pieces

Use these pieces to solve the *Dissection Puzzles* in the *Student Guide.*

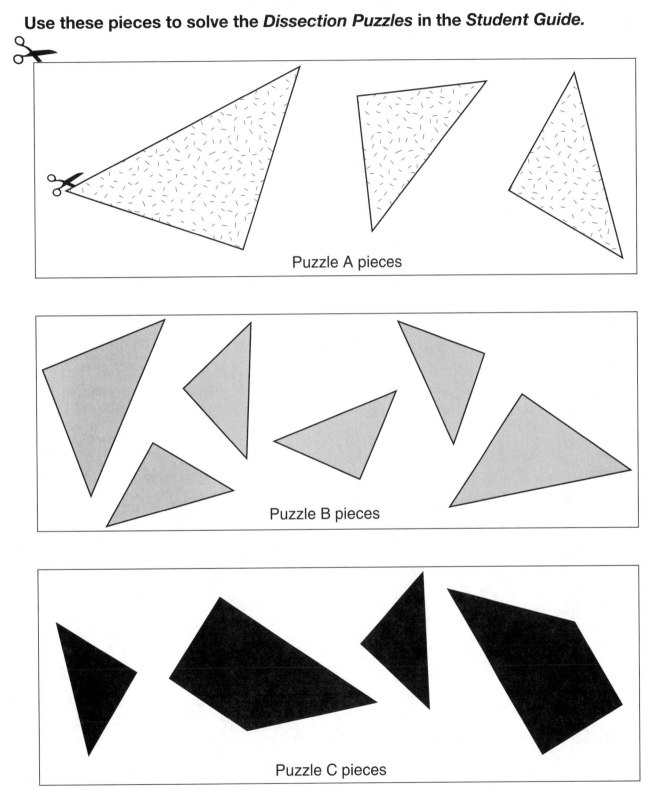

Puzzle A pieces

Puzzle B pieces

Puzzle C pieces

Hex

Players

This is a game for two players, Player X and Player O.

Materials

- two kinds of small markers (Two different kinds of beans work well.)

Rules

1. On each turn a player places a marker on any empty hexagon.

2. Player X wins when there is a path that connects the two sides of the board that have Xs.

3. Player O wins when there is a path that connects the two sides of the board that have Os.

4. There is always a winner.

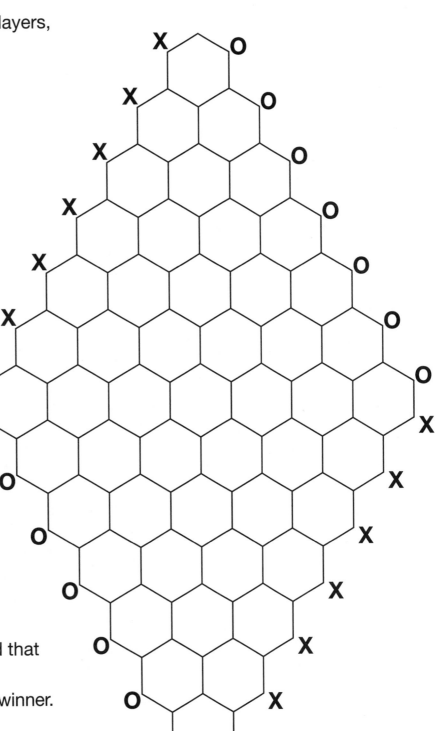

Unit 13

Parts and Wholes

	Student Guide	Discovery Assignment Book	Adventure Book	Unit Resource Guide*
Lesson 1				
Kid Fractions	●			
Lesson 2				
What's 1?	●	●		●
Lesson 3				
Pizza Problems	●			●
Lesson 4				
Fraction Games	●	●		
Lesson 5				
Fraction Problems	●			

Unit Resource Guide pages are from the teacher materials.

Unit 13 Home Practice

PART 1

1. Ms. O'Neil has 25 students in her third-grade class. One-fifth go home for lunch, two-fifths bring a sack lunch, and two-fifths buy a hot lunch at school. Use beans or other counters to help you.

   A. What number of students go home for lunch? _____

   B. What number of students bring a lunch to school? _____

   C. What number of students buy a lunch at school? _____

2. Mr. Dwyer has 24 students in his third-grade class. 1/4 take the bus to school, 2/4 walk to school, and 1/4 get a ride in a car.

   A. What number of students take the bus to school? _____

   B. What number of students walk to school? _____

   C. What number of students get a ride in a car? _____

PART 2

1. Skip count by thirds to 10. Write the numbers.

$\frac{1}{3}$	$\frac{1}{3}$	$\frac{1}{3}$	$\frac{1}{3}$	$\frac{1}{3}$	$\frac{1}{3}$	$\frac{1}{3}$	$\frac{1}{3}$	$\frac{1}{3}$
$\frac{1}{3}$	$\frac{2}{3}$	1	$1\frac{1}{3}$	$1\frac{2}{3}$	2	$2\frac{1}{3}$	$2\frac{2}{3}$	3

_____

_____

2. I am $\frac{1}{3}$ more than 1. What number am I? _____

3. I am $\frac{1}{3}$ less than 1. What number am I? _____

4. I am $\frac{1}{3}$ more than $1\frac{1}{3}$. What number am I? _____

5. I am $\frac{1}{3}$ more than $1\frac{2}{3}$. What number am I? _____

Name _____ Date _____

PART 3

Use a clock and a calculator to help you solve these problems.

How many minutes are there in:

1. 2 hours? _____

2. $1\frac{1}{2}$ hours? _____

3. $1\frac{1}{4}$ hours? _____

4. $1\frac{3}{4}$ hours? _____

5. $2\frac{1}{2}$ hours? _____

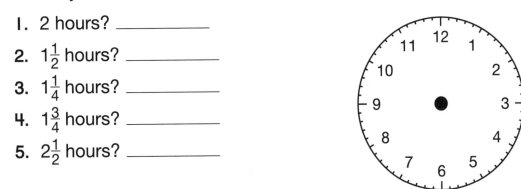

PART 4

Use what you know about quarters and $\frac{1}{4}$s to solve these problems. Tell how much money you would have after adding or subtracting these amounts.

1. You have 25¢ more than $2.50. _____

2. You have 25¢ less than $2.50. _____

3. You have 50¢ more than $2.50. _____

4. You have $1.50 more than $3.50. _____

5. You have $2.00 less than $3.75. _____

PART 5

Solve the problems. Estimate to be sure your answers are reasonable.

| 1. | 4006
 +498 | 2. | 4006
 −498 | 3. | 7032
 +1777 | 4. | 7032
 −1779 |

5. Explain your estimation strategy for Question 2.

Triangle Flash Cards: Square Numbers

- Work with a partner. Each partner cuts out the flash cards.
- Your partner chooses one card at a time and covers the shaded number.
- Multiply the two uncovered numbers.
- Divide the cards into three piles: those facts you know and can answer quickly, those you can figure out with a strategy, and those you need to learn.
- Practice the last two piles again. Then make a list of the facts you need to practice at home.
- Repeat the directions for your partner.

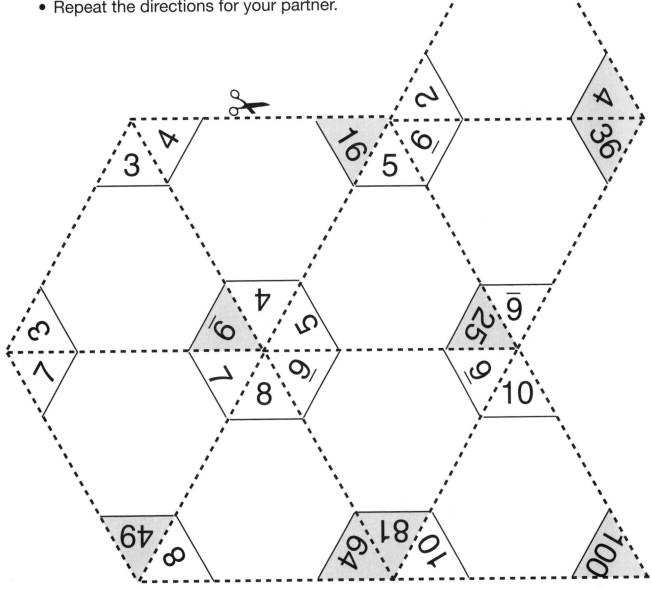

Naming Wholes and Parts

Solve the following problems.

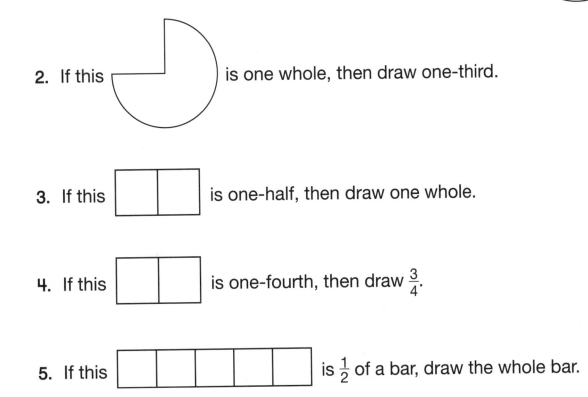

1. Stephanie, Simon, and Caroline want to share this leftover pizza fairly. Draw how much pizza each person should get.

2. If this [shape] is one whole, then draw one-third.

3. If this [shape] is one-half, then draw one whole.

4. If this [shape] is one-fourth, then draw $\frac{3}{4}$.

5. If this [shape] is $\frac{1}{2}$ of a bar, draw the whole bar.

The next few problems are about a very important fraction, one-half. Use the back of this page for your answers.

6. Show one-half using a rectangle.

7. Show one-half using a circle.

8. Make up a story problem with one-half in it.

9. List some fractions that equal one-half.

FractionLand Whole
Number Deck

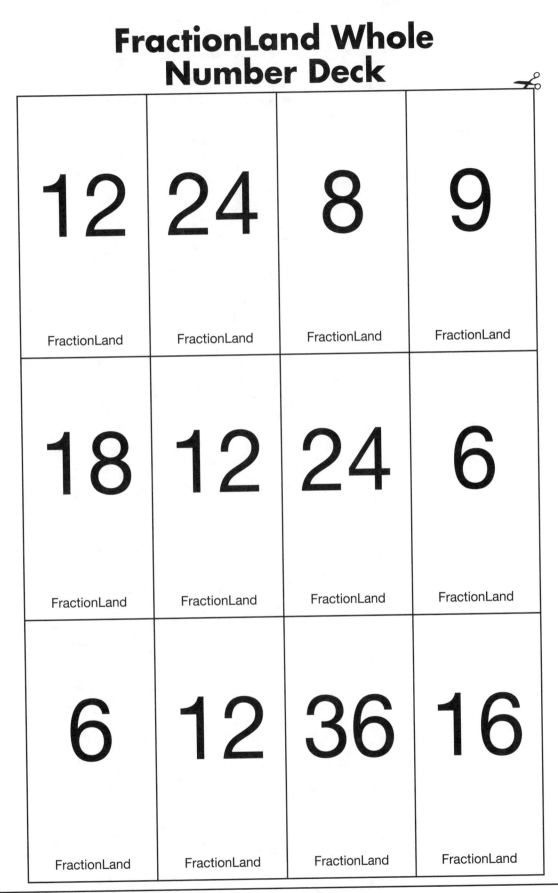

12	24	8	9
FractionLand	FractionLand	FractionLand	FractionLand
18	12	24	6
FractionLand	FractionLand	FractionLand	FractionLand
6	12	36	16
FractionLand	FractionLand	FractionLand	FractionLand

FractionLand Fraction Deck

$\dfrac{1}{2}$	$\dfrac{1}{3}$	$\dfrac{1}{4}$	$\dfrac{3}{4}$
FractionLand	FractionLand	FractionLand	FractionLand
$\dfrac{1}{2}$	$\dfrac{1}{3}$	$\dfrac{1}{4}$	$\dfrac{3}{4}$
FractionLand	FractionLand	FractionLand	FractionLand
$\dfrac{0}{3}$	$\dfrac{3}{3}$	$\dfrac{2}{3}$	$\dfrac{2}{3}$
FractionLand	FractionLand	FractionLand	FractionLand

FractionLand Game Board

Start			**24** Go $\frac{1}{4}$ of the way back.	**25** Go ahead $\frac{2}{5}$ of 25.	**26** Take another turn.	
1			**23**		**27**	
2			**22** Take another turn.		**28**	**29**
3 Go ahead $\frac{2}{3}$ of 3.	**4** Go ahead $\frac{1}{2}$ of 4.		**21** Go ahead $\frac{1}{3}$ of 21.		**30** Go $\frac{1}{3}$ of the way back.	
	5		**20**	**19**	**31**	
7	**6**			**18**	**32**	
8 Take another turn.		**15** Go $\frac{2}{3}$ of the way back.	**16** Go ahead $\frac{1}{8}$ of 16.	**17**	**33**	
9 Go ahead $\frac{1}{3}$ of 9.						
10 Go $\frac{3}{10}$ of the way back.	**14** Go $\frac{1}{2}$ of the way back.			**34**		
11	**12**	**13**		**36**	**35**	
				Finish		

Fraction Problem Game
Fraction Cards

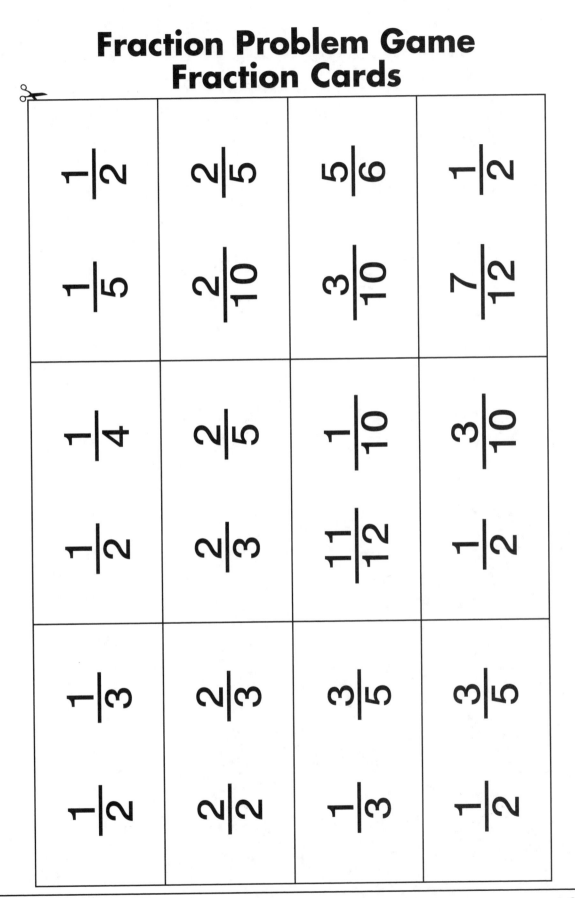

Fraction Problem Game Helper

Use these circles and fractions to help you compare fraction sizes in *Fraction Problem Game.*

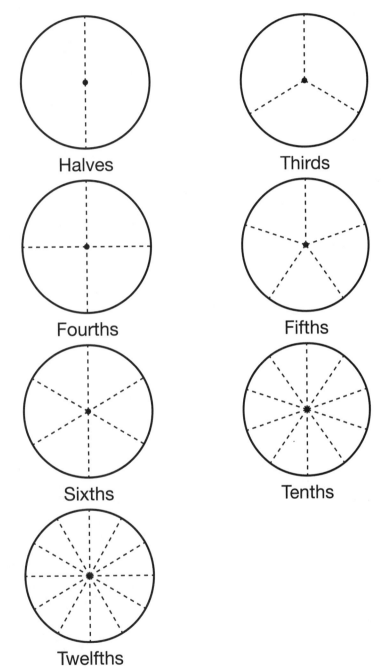

Halves

Thirds

Fourths

Fifths

Sixths

Tenths

Twelfths

Fraction Games

Problem Game Board

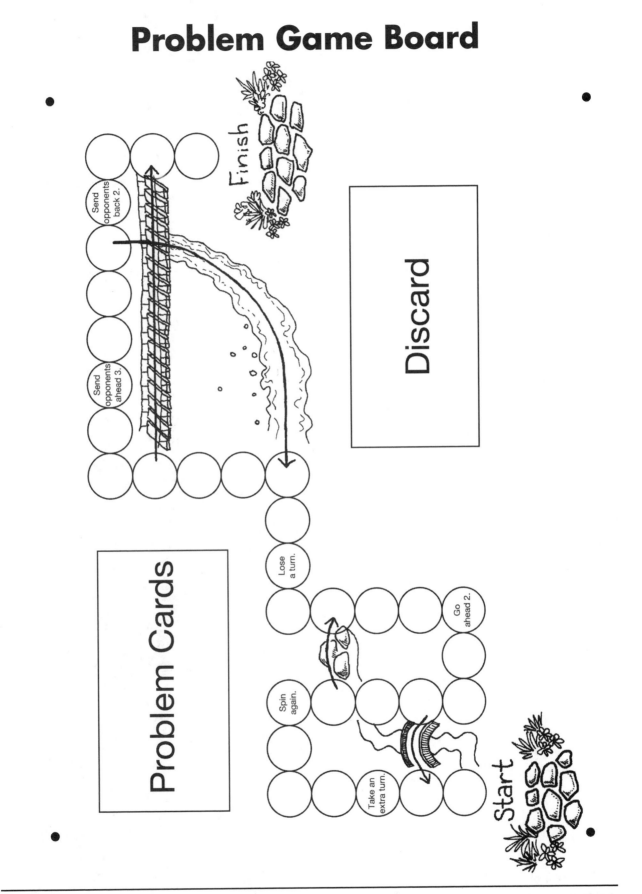

Problem Game Spinner

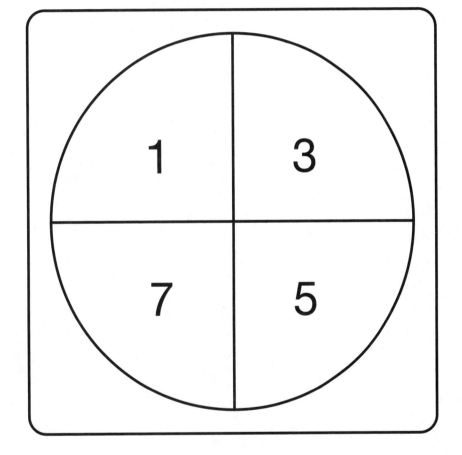

Unit 14

Collecting and Using Data

	Student Guide	Discovery Assignment Book	Adventure Book	Unit Resource Guide*
Lesson 1				
Time Again	●			●
Lesson 2				
Time and Time Again	●	●		
Lesson 3				
Tracking Our Reading	●			
Lesson 4				
Make Your Own Survey	●			
Lesson 5				
Reviewing Addition and Subtraction	●			●

*Unit Resource Guide pages are from the teacher materials.

Unit 14 Home Practice

PART 1

1. 82 + 69 = _____

2. 472 + 579 = _____

3. 8 × 200 = _____

4. 300 × 5 = _____

5. Find two 2-digit numbers with a sum of 137. _____ and _____

6. The normal temperature for July in Nome, Alaska, is 51°F. In Phoenix, Arizona, it is 92°F.

   A. Usually, how many degrees warmer is it in Phoenix than in Nome for the month of July? _____

   B. What is the normal temperature in San Francisco, California, for July if it is 13 degrees warmer than the normal temperature in Nome? _____

   C. What is the normal temperature in San Antonio, Texas, for July if it is 44 degrees warmer than Nome? _____

PART 2

1. 665 – 456 = _____

2. 604 – 456 = _____

3. 350 + 50 + _____ = 1000

4. 1000 – 350 = _____

5. 250 + 400 + _____ = 1000

6. 1000 – 250 = _____

7. 420 + 100 + _____ = 1000

8. 1000 – 420 = _____

9. Nick's family had to drive 143 miles to visit his grandma for Thanksgiving. Nick asked, "Are we there yet?" His dad said, "We have about 47 miles to go." About how many miles had they driven already?

_____

COLLECTING AND USING DATA

PART 3

1. How many hops, starting at 0, will it take a +9 mathhopper to pass

   80? _____ What number will it land on? _____

2. Measure the perimeter of the rectangle below to the nearest half of a

   centimeter. _____

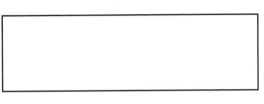

3. How many rectangles are in the figure below? _____

PART 4

1. How many 30-minute periods are there from 3:00 P.M. until 10:00 P.M.?

   _____

2. Nine hundred fifty-two is . . .

   A. 100 more than _____   **B.** 50 more than _____

   C. 50 less than _____   **D.** about twice _____

3. Find one way that you can divide five $100 bills, eight $50 bills, and
   five $20 bills into two equal shares.

   _____

   _____

Triangle Flash Cards: 9s

- Work with a partner. Each partner cuts out the 9 flash cards.
- Your partner chooses one card at a time and covers the shaded number.
- Multiply the two uncovered numbers.
- Divide the cards into three piles: those facts you know and can answer quickly, those you can figure out with a strategy, and those you need to learn.
- Practice the last two piles again. Then make a list of the facts you need to practice at home.
- Repeat the directions for your partner.

Time and Time Again
Analog Cards

Time and Time Again

Time and Time Again

Time and Time Again

Time and Time Again

Time and Time Again

Time and Time Again

Time and Time Again

Time and Time Again

Time and Time Again

Time and Time Again

Time and Time Again

Time and Time Again

Time and Time Again | Time and Time Again | Time and Time Again | Time and Time Again

Time and Time Again | Time and Time Again | Time and Time Again | Time and Time Again

Time and Time Again | Time and Time Again | Time and Time Again | Time and Time Again

Time and Time Again
Digital Cards

3:00	**4:30**	**11:45**	**8:15**
Time and Time Again	Time and Time Again	Time and Time Again	Time and Time Again
7:05	**3:55**	**8:50**	**11:20**
Time and Time Again	Time and Time Again	Time and Time Again	Time and Time Again
1:25	**3:10**	**5:35**	**10:40**
Time and Time Again	Time and Time Again	Time and Time Again	Time and Time Again

5:55	10:00	12:15	6:45
Time and Time Again	Time and Time Again	Time and Time Again	Time and Time Again
3:50	8:20	9:05	11:25
Time and Time Again	Time and Time Again	Time and Time Again	Time and Time Again
12:35	2:55	4:45	2:15
Time and Time Again	Time and Time Again	Time and Time Again	Time and Time Again

Unit 15

Decimal Investigations

	Student Guide	Discovery Assignment Book	Adventure Book	Unit Resource Guide*
Lesson 1				
Decimal Fractions	●	●		
Lesson 2				
Measuring to the Nearest Tenth	●	●		●
Lesson 3				
Decimal Hex		●		
Lesson 4				
Length vs. Number	●			
Lesson 5				
Nothing to It!	●			

Unit Resource Guide pages are from the teacher materials.

(Unit 15) Home Practice

PART 1

1. 358
   + 9

2. 358
   + 89

3. 358
   +789

4. 900
   −468

5. 900
   −567

6. 900
   −366

7. Below are the heights of three buildings in Cincinnati, Ohio.

   The Carew Tower: 568 feet
   Central Trust Tower: 504 feet
   Dubois Tower: 423 feet

   If these three towers were stacked to form one tower, it would be 41 feet taller than the Sears Tower (without its antennas) in Chicago.

   How tall is the Sears Tower? _____

PART 2

1. 5550
   − 8

2. 5550
   − 68

3. 5550
   − 468

4. 5550
   −2468

5. Tina collects pennies. After she gave her brother 65 pennies she had 289 pennies. How many pennies did Tina start with?

   _____

6. At the circus there were eight clowns, and each clown was juggling four bowling pins. How many bowling pins were there?

   _____

PART 3

1. A line segment is a piece of a line. Measure the line segment below to the nearest tenth of a centimeter. _____ cm

    |———————————————————————————|

2. Draw line segments that measure 3 cm, 6.5 cm, and 12 cm.

    3 cm:

    6.5 cm:

    12 cm:

3. A. Is more or less than $\frac{1}{2}$ of the rectangle shaded? _____

    B. Is more or less than $\frac{1}{3}$ shaded? _____

    C. Is more or less than $\frac{1}{4}$ shaded? _____

PART 4

1. Is $\frac{1}{5}$ the same as 1.5? Why or why not? Explain in words or with a picture.

2. Let the flat be one whole and the skinny be one-tenth. Show these amounts with base-ten shorthand.

    A. 1.9 _____

    B. 0.5 _____

    C. 4.2 _____

    D. 2.0 _____

Triangle Flash Cards:
The Last Six Facts

- Work with a partner. Cut out the flash cards.
- Your partner chooses one card at a time and covers the shaded number. Multiply the two uncovered numbers.
- Divide the cards into three piles: those facts you know and can answer quickly, those you can figure out with a strategy, and those you need to learn.
- Practice the last two piles again. Then make a list of the facts you need to practice at home.
- Repeat the directions for your partner.

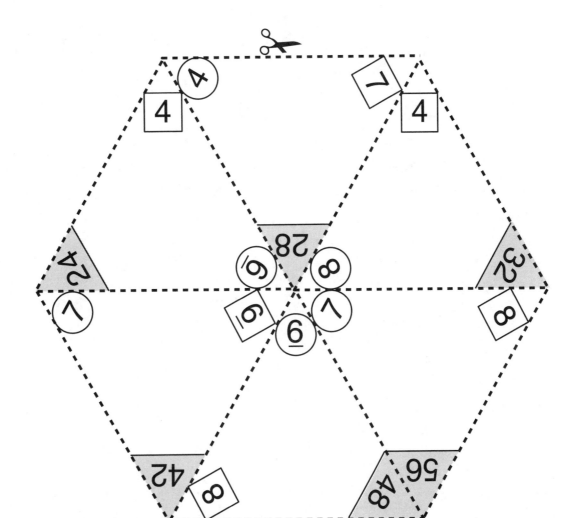

Tenths Helper

Place skinnies on this chart to find how many tenths are in one whole and two wholes. Skip count by tenths.

Tenths Table

Complete the table below. You will need base-ten pieces. For this page, the flat is one whole. Use the Fewest Pieces Rule when writing decimal fractions.

Base-Ten Shorthand	Fraction of a Flat	
	Common	**Decimal**
1. □ /|/|	$1\frac{4}{10}$	1.4
2. □ □ |//|/| /|		
3.		0.3
4. |//|/||//|/||//	$\frac{15}{10}$	
5.	$\frac{23}{10}$	
6. □ |//|/|		
7. □ □ □ |//|/||//|		

Decimal Fractions

Decimal Hunt

Homework

Dear Family Member:

Your child is learning about decimals in class. As homework, we ask that your child find examples of decimals at home. This will help your child make connections between lessons in school and the real world. It will also provide us with interesting examples to discuss in class.

Thank you for your help.

Look for decimals at home and in your neighborhood. You might look on boxes and cans of food or in newspapers and magazines. Try to find at least six decimals. If you can, cut out the paper or label with the decimal on it.

Write about each decimal you find. Tell where you found it, and try to explain what it means. If you can, tell what one whole is for each decimal.

For example, you might find 0.347 L on a bottle. This means that the whole is 1 liter. The decimal tells what fraction of a liter the bottle holds.

Measure Hunt

Look for objects that would go in each of the tables below. Then record their metric measurements. Write which way you made each measurement: length, width, height, diameter, and so on. When it makes sense, try to measure to the nearest tenth of a centimeter.

Objects less than 2 cm

Object	Measurement	Which way?

Objects between 5 and 10 cm

Object	Measurement	Which way?

Objects between 20 and 30 cm

Object	Measurement	Which way?

Objects between 110 and 130 cm

Object	Measurement	Which way?

Decimal Hex

Players

This is a game for two or three players.

Materials

- *Decimal Hex Game Board*
- two same color centimeter cubes or other markers for each player
- one clear plastic spinner or pencil and paper clip

Rules

The goal of this game is to move two cubes or other markers from matching hexagons to opposite matching hexagons that have the same number.

1. Each player places both of his or her cubes on two matching hexagons on one side of the game board. The target hexagons are the matching ones on the other side of the game board.
2. The first player spins the spinner.
3. If "Greater Than or Equal To" shows, the player may move one cube to a neighboring hexagon with a number that is greater than or equal to the number in the hexagon where the cube is now.
4. If "Less Than or Equal To" shows, the player may move one cube to a neighboring hexagon with a number that is less than or equal to the number in the hexagon where the cube is now.
5. The player may not be able to move a cube during his or her turn.
6. More than one cube can be on the same hexagon at the same time.
7. Players take turns spinning the spinner and moving cubes.
8. The first player to get **both** cubes to his or her target hexagons is the winner.

Decimal Hex Game Board

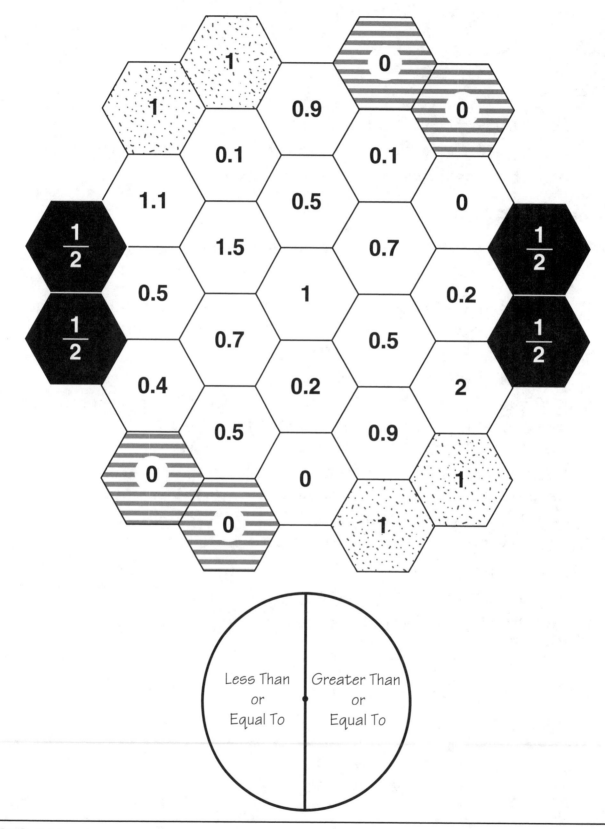

Unit 16

Volume

	Student Guide	Discovery Assignment Book	Adventure Book	Unit Resource Guide*
Lesson 1				
Measuring Volume	●			
Lesson 2				
Fill 'er Up!	●			
Lesson 3				
Volume Hunt		●		
Lesson 4				
Elixir of Youth			●	
Lesson 5				
Paying Taxes Problems	●			

Unit Resource Guide pages are from the teacher materials.

Name _____ Date _____

Unit 16 Home Practice

PART 1

1. 95
  + 66

2. 395
  + 766

3. 72
  − 46

4. 6020
  − 3561

5. John brought 36 baseball cards to a birthday party. This is a little less than half of his collection. About how many cards could John have in his collection?

_____

6. Nick has 97 baseball cards. A little less than half of these are from his father's collection. About how many of Nick's cards are from his dad?

_____

PART 2

1. Find all the pairs of numbers in the circle that have a sum of 100. Write a number sentence for each sum.

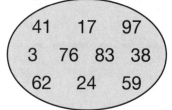

41   17   97
3   76   83   38
62   24   59

2. What number does each arrow point to (to nearest tenth of a cm)?

A = _____   B = _____   C = _____   D = _____

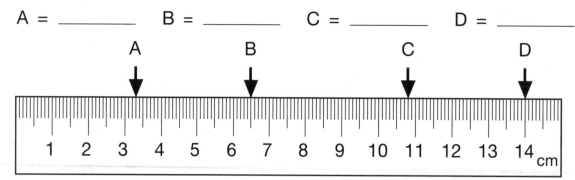

VOLUME

PART 3

1. You are given a balance and some 8-gram, 5-gram, and 1-gram masses. How many of each would you need to balance an object with a mass of 78 grams? Show your work.

_____

_____

2. A graduated cylinder is filled with 40 cc of water. Four marbles of the same size are added to the cylinder. The level of the water rises to 52 cc. What is the volume of each marble? Show your work.

_____

_____

3. Tanya's parents told her that if she can save $100.00 towards a new bike, they will pay the rest. So far she has saved $20.00. She makes $9.00 every Saturday baby-sitting. How many weeks will it take Tanya to save $100.00? Show your work.

_____

_____

PART 4

1. How many hops will a +2 mathhopper take to reach or go past 100 if it starts on 0? Show your work on a piece of paper. _____

2. How many hops will a +5 mathhopper need to take to reach 1000 if it starts at 0? Show your work on a piece of paper. _____

3. If a +10 mathhopper starts at 5 and takes 8 hops, on what number will it land? Show your work on a piece of paper. _____

Volume Hunt

At Home

1. Find two containers of different sizes: 1 cup, 1 pint, 1 quart, or 1 gallon. Fill the smaller container with water, and empty it into the larger container. How many times can you do this without making the larger container overflow?

2. If your smaller container is a cup, answer Question 2A.

   If your smaller container is a pint, answer Question 2B.

   If your smaller container is a quart, answer Question 2C.

   A. How many cups are in a _____?

   size of larger container

   _____ cups

   B. How many pints are in a _____?

   size of larger container

   _____ pints

   C. How many quarts are in a _____?

   size of larger container

   _____ quarts

In Class

Share your findings with your classmates.

3. Fill in the answers in the unshaded boxes in the table below. You can use arithmetic to help you complete the table.

Converting Standard Volume Units

	cup	pint	quart	gallon
number of cups in a				
number of pints in a				
number of quarts in a				
number of gallons in a				

4. How many cups are in 2 pints? _____

5. How many quarts are in 3 gallons? _____

6. How many cups are in 5 quarts? _____

Unit 17

Wholes and Parts

	Student Guide	Discovery Assignment Book	Adventure Book	Unit Resource Guide*
Lesson 1 Geoboard Fractions	●			●
Lesson 2 Folding Fractions	●	●		●
Lesson 3 The Clever Tailor			●	
Lesson 4 Fraction Hex		●		

*Unit Resource Guide pages are from the teacher materials.

Unit 17 **Home Practice**

PART 1

Use your estimating skills to help you solve the following problems.

1. 87
   $+ 50$

2. 87
   $+ 58$

3. 94
   $- 30$

4. 94
   $- 27$

5. Which two numbers below should you add if you want an answer:

   77   **85**   **26**   **48**

   A. over 150? _____

   B. very close to 100? _____

   Which two numbers should you subtract if you want an answer:

   C. close to 25? _____

   D. less than 10? _____

PART 2

1. 335
   $+ 47$

2. 474
   $+ 96$

3. 6931
   $- 289$

4. 7030
   $- 3441$

5. Explain a strategy for solving Question 2 using mental math.

6. In a jump-a-thon for heart disease, Linda jumped rope 42 times without tripping. Carol jumped 33 times. Michael jumped 38 times.

   A. Did this group jump more or less than 100 times? _____

   B. One sponsor agreed to pay the group of three 10¢ for each jump. How much money did they earn from the sponsor?

WHOLES AND PARTS

PART 3

Use these pictures to answer Questions 1 and 2.

A.

B.

C.

1. What fraction of each rectangle above is shaded?

   A. _____   B. _____   C. _____

2. Are the shaded parts of each rectangle more than 50%, less than 50%, or equal to 50% of the whole rectangle?

   A. _____   B. _____   C. _____

Use this picture to answer Questions 3 and 4.

3. Area of the large square = _____

4. Area of shaded triangle = _____

PART 4

1. If this is 1 cubic centimeter: , what is the volume of A and B?

   A. _____   B. _____

2. Draw 18 squares on a separate piece of paper (or use grid paper).

   A. Color 1/2 of the 18 squares red.

   B. Color 1/3 of the 18 squares blue.

   C. Color 1/6 of the 18 squares green.

Folding Fractions Data Tables

One-third

Colored Parts	Total Parts	Fraction Colored

One-half

Colored Parts	Total Parts	Fraction Colored

One-fourth

Colored Parts	Total Parts	Fraction Colored

Folding Fractions

Fraction Hex

Players

This is a game for two or three players.

Materials

- *Fraction Hex Game Board*
- two same color centimeter cubes or other markers for each player
- one clear plastic spinner or pencil and paper clip

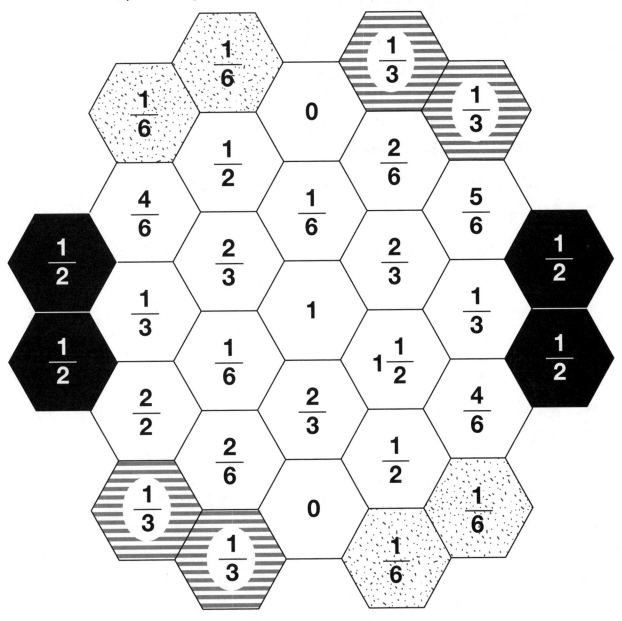

Rules

The goal of this game is to move two cubes or other game markers from matching hexagons to opposite matching hexagons that have the same number.

1. Each player places both of his or her cubes on two matching hexagons on one side of the game board. The target hexagons are the matching ones on the other side of the game board.

2. The first player spins the spinner.

3. If "Greater Than or Equal To" shows, the player may move one cube to a neighboring hexagon with a number that is greater than or equal to the number in the hexagon where the cube is now.

4. If "Less Than or Equal To" shows, the player may move one cube to a neighboring hexagon with a number that is less than or equal to the number in the hexagon where the cube is now.

5. The player may not be able to move a cube during his or her turn.

6. More than one cube can be on the same hexagon at the same time.

7. Players take turns spinning the spinner and moving cubes.

8. The first player to get **both** cubes to his or her target hexagons is the winner.

Use pattern blocks or these pictures to compare fractions.

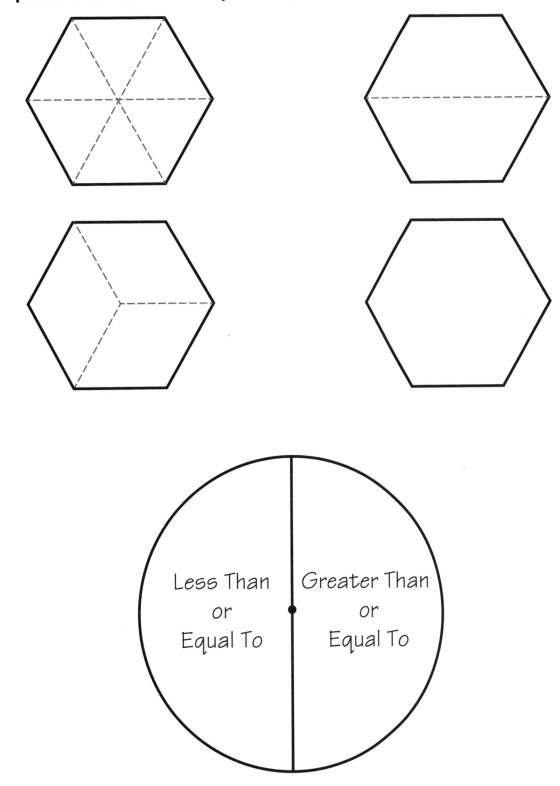

Unit 18

Viewing and Drawing 3-D

	Student Guide	Discovery Assignment Book	Adventure Book	Unit Resource Guide*
Lesson 1				
Viewing 3-D Objects	●			
Lesson 2				
Drawing 3-D Objects	●	●		
Lesson 3				
Building and Planning Cube Models	●			●
Lesson 4				
Top, Front, and Right Side Views	●			●
Lesson 5				
Problems with Shapes	●			●

Unit Resource Guide pages are from the teacher materials.

Unit 18 Home Practice

PART 1

1. $150 - 90 = $ _____

2. $110 - 90 = $ _____

3. $130 - 90 = $ _____

4. $75 + $ _____ $= 120$

5. $500 - $ _____ $= 380$

6. $46 + $ _____ $= 100$

7. Helen's family went canoeing. The canoe's label read: "Maximum load: 350 pounds." Helen's dad weighs 183 pounds. Helen weighs 68 pounds. What's the heaviest a third person can be if he or she rides with Helen and her dad? Show your work.

_____

_____

PART 2

1. $800 + 800 = $ _____

2. $800 + 900 = $ _____

3. $700 + 800 = $ _____

4. $\begin{array}{r} 802 \\ +799 \\ \hline \end{array}$

5. $\begin{array}{r} 815 \\ +885 \\ \hline \end{array}$

6. $\begin{array}{r} 687 \\ +836 \\ \hline \end{array}$

7. Explain a way to solve Question 4 using mental math.

8. Lake Superior, which is the longest Great Lake, is 350 miles long. It is 157 miles longer than Lake Ontario. How long is Lake Ontario?

VIEWING AND DRAWING 3-D

PART 3

1. What units can be used to measure:

   A. the length of your finger? _____

   B. the area of your hand? _____

   C. the volume of a cereal box? _____

2. What is the volume of the cube model which is built using this plan?

   _____

4	3	4
2	1	4

3. Make a different cube model plan on a sheet of paper. Keep the volume the same as in Question 2. You may change the floor plan.

PART 4

1. Skip count by fives backwards from 80. Record the numbers below as you say them.

   _____

   _____

2. Skip count by fours backwards from 60. Record the numbers.

   _____

   _____

3. $6 \times 3 =$ _____   4. $6 \times 30 =$ _____   5. $6 \times 300 =$ _____

6. Explain how you would find the answer to 6×29. _____

   _____

   _____

Working with Cubes

1. Here is a picture of a box that is a cube.

   How many faces do you see? _____

2. Trace the edges. How many edges did you trace? _____

3. Describe the shapes of the faces you traced.

   A. How many edges does each face have?

   B. Did the artist draw any right angles? If so, how many?

   _____

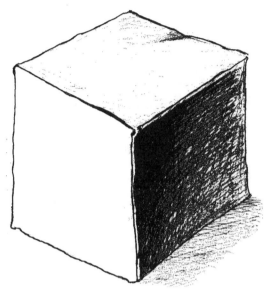

4. Name the shapes you traced. Are they quadrilaterals? squares? parallelograms?

   _____

5. Below is a 2-D drawing that represents a cube.

   How many faces do you see? _____

6. Trace the edges. How many edges did you trace? _____

7. Describe the shapes of the faces you traced.

   A. How many edges does each face have?

   B. Did the artist draw any right angles? If so, how many?

   _____

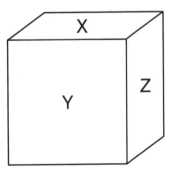

8. Name the shapes of the faces you traced in this 2-D drawing.

   _____

9. Here is Cara's sketch of a cube.

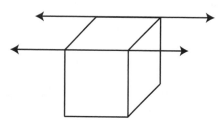

A. She has traced two edges that are parallel to one another. Find and trace a third edge that is parallel to the first two.

B. Find two more sets of three edges that are parallel to one another. Trace one set of parallel edges with one color pen or pencil and trace the other set with another color.

10. Now it's your turn to draw a cube. Below is a square. Use it as the front face of your cube drawing.

Plan your drawing before you start. Here are some questions to think about before you start drawing.

A. How many more edges will you need to draw?

B. Which edges should be parallel?

C. What shapes will you draw to show the other two faces?

Drawing Rectangular Prisms

1. Here is a sketch of a box of Keenya's favorite cereal. Trace the edges in the sketch.

2. Try to draw your own cereal box. Plan your drawing before you start. Here are some things to think about before you start.

   A. How many edges will you need to draw?

   B. Which edges should be parallel?

   C. What shapes will you draw to show the three faces?

Unit 19

Multiplication and Division Problems

	Student Guide	Discovery Assignment Book	Adventure Book	Unit Resource Guide*
Lesson 1				
Break-apart Products	●			
Lesson 2				
More Multiplication Stories	●			
Lesson 3				
Making Groups				
Lesson 4				
Solving Problems with Division	●			●

Unit Resource Guide pages are from the teacher materials.

Unit 19 Home Practice

PART 1

Tell whether the sum of each is more than 600, less than 600, or equal to 600.

1. 300 + 300 _____

2. 318 + 264 _____

3. 268 + 295 _____

4. 329 + 282 _____

5. 240 + 360 _____

6. 363 + 302 _____

Fill in the blanks below so each number sentence equals 1000.

7. _____ + _____ + 300 = 1000

8. _____ + 150 + _____ = 1000

9. 335 + _____ + _____ = 1000

PART 2

1.	2.	3.	4.	5.	6.
79 + 69	979 − 430	75 × 4	32 × 9	60 × 4	83 × 7

7. Find two 3-digit numbers whose sum is 251. _____

_____

8. Find two numbers whose difference is 79. _____

_____

MULTIPLICATION AND DIVISION PROBLEMS

PART 3

1. Draw a rectangle, a pentagon, and a hexagon on paper. Draw the pentagon with the largest area, and the rectangle with the smallest area. You do not have to find the exact area of each shape. Use a ruler to make your drawings.

2. Michael measured his height. He said to his mom, "I am 48." She said, "No, you're not. You're 8!" How could Michael and his mother have avoided this misunderstanding?

   _____

   _____

3. Measure and record the perimeter of a table top in your home. Draw a picture of the table you measured and show the length of each side. Remember to include the units.

   _____

4. List the following measurements in order from shortest to longest.

   5 inches, 5 meters, 5 cm

   _____

PART 4

1. Write a story and draw a picture about $\frac{1}{4} \times 20$ on a sheet of paper. Write a number sentence on your picture.

2. How many 10-gram masses would it take to balance a 120-gram object?

3. A +6 mathhopper takes 60 hops, starting at 0. Where does it land? If it takes 63 hops, where does it land?

4.
   A. 96
       × 2

   B. 64
       × 8

   C. 40
       × 7

   D. 47
       × 3

Unit 20

Connections:
An Assessment Unit

	Student Guide	Discovery Assignment Book	Adventure Book	Unit Resource Guide*
Lesson 1				
Experiment Review	●			
Lesson 2				
Tower Power		●		
Lesson 3				
Becca's Towers				●
Lesson 4				
Earning Money				●
Lesson 5				
End-of-Year Test				●

Unit Resource Guide pages are from the teacher materials.

Unit 20 **Home Practice**

PART 1

1.	2.	3.	4.
70 × 9	877 + 549	51 × 8	551 − 435

5. $400 - 237 =$ _____   6. $719 + 281 =$ _____   7. $46 \times 3 =$ _____

8. In the morning, Alex spends 25 minutes getting ready for school, an hour delivering papers, and 15 minutes walking to school. If Alex must be at school by 8:00, what time should he wake up?

Show your work. _____

_____

PART 2

1.	2.	3.	4.	5.	6.
893 − 5	893 − 95	893 − 495	645 + 6	645 + 86	645 + 986

7. Explain a strategy for solving Question 2 in your head.

8. **A.** At the movies, Roberto's mom spent $5.75 on two drinks and one bag of popcorn. If each drink costs $1.75, how much did the popcorn cost?

   B. If she paid with a ten-dollar bill, how much change should Roberto's mom get back?

PART 3

1. Four 8-gram masses, three 5-gram masses, and three 1-gram masses balance an object. What is the mass of the object?

   _____

2. A. Name something at home that is about 15 inches long.

   _____

   B. Name something that is about 15 cm long. _____

   C. Name something that is about one meter long. _____

3. A graduated cylinder is filled with water, six marbles of the same size are added, and the level of the water rises to 54 cc. Each marble has a volume of 4 cc. How much water is in the cylinder?

   _____

PART 4

1. Which number is the largest? Which is smallest? Explain how you know. $\dfrac{13}{10}$ 2/10   0.9

   _____

2. You are going to have a party. 1/2 of your guests will be relatives, 1/4 will be classmates, and 1/4 will be neighbors. Plan how many people you will invite. Draw a picture on paper and label it clearly.

3. A. At midnight on New Year's Eve, 50% of the 70 balloons at a party were popped by the guests. How many balloons were popped?

   _____

   B. Five children divided the rest of the balloons. How many balloons did each child get? _____

Triangle Flash Card Master

- Make a flash card for each fact that is not circled on your *Multiplication Facts I Know* chart. Write the largest number (the product) in the shaded corner of each triangle. Then cut out the flash cards.
- To quiz you on a multiplication fact, your partner covers the shaded number. Multiply the two uncovered numbers.
- Repeat the directions for your partner.

Triangle Flash Card Master

- Make a flash card for each fact that is not circled on your *Multiplication Facts I Know* chart. Write the largest number (the product) in the shaded corner of each triangle. Then cut out the flash cards.
- To quiz you on a multiplication fact, your partner covers the shaded number. Multiply the two uncovered numbers.
- Repeat the directions for your partner.

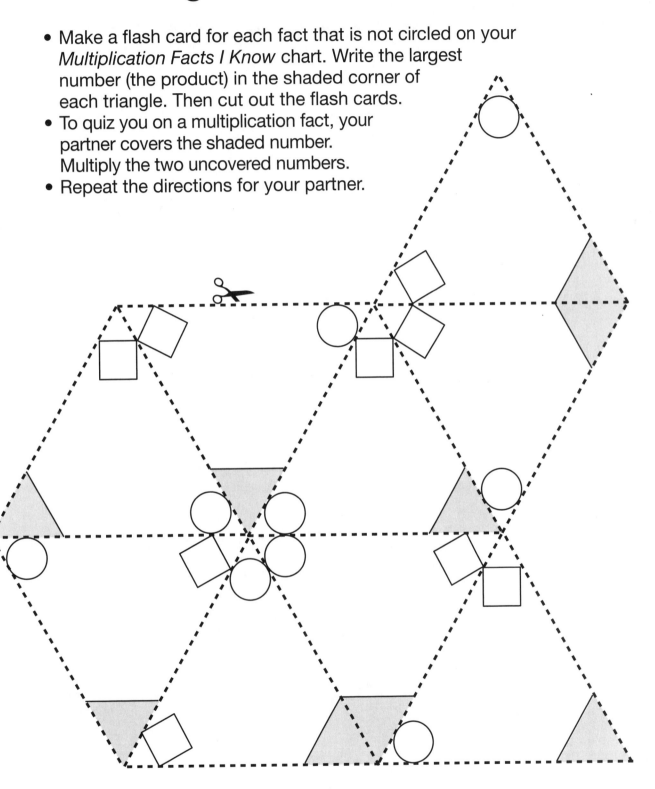

Tower Power

The mayor has hired you to be an architect for Tiny TIMS Town. You are part of a team that will design a new office tower. The design for the tower must follow the instructions below:

- The area of the base of the tower is 6 square centimeters.

- The floor plan for each floor of the tower must be exactly the same.

Your floor plan does not need to have this shape, but the area must be 6 square centimeters. To prepare for building your Tiny TIMS Town Tower, you will have 40 centimeter connecting cubes to build tower models of various heights. (They will be shorter than the tower shown in the picture.) Your team must first design a Tower Floor Plan. Each of the models you build must use the same Tower Floor Plan.

You will collect data about the towers you build. This data will help you predict the volume of a tower if you know the height of the tower and the area of its base.

I. **A.** What three variables are important in this lab? _____

   _____

   B. When you build your towers and record the data, which two of

   these variables will change? _____

   C. Which variable will stay the same? _____

Draw your group's Tower Floor Plan. Write the area of your Tower Floor Plan on your drawing. You will be adding to this drawing later.

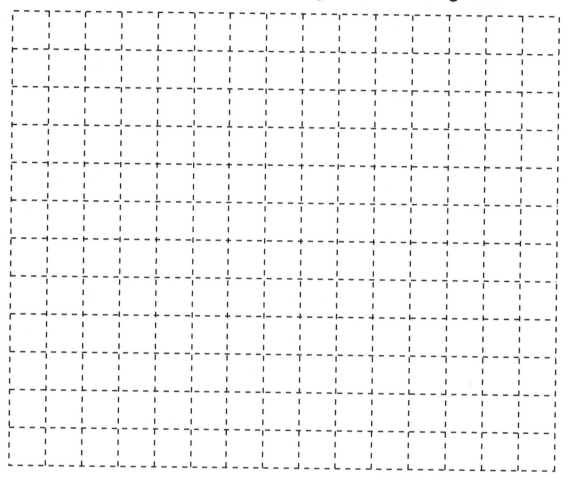

Using your Tower Floor Plan, build at least three towers of different heights. You can do this in either of these ways:

- You can build one tower at a time. Before building your next tower, record the height and volume for the tower, take it apart, and build your next tower.

- If you have enough centimeter connecting cubes, you can build all three towers at once.

Record the height and volume of each tower. Label your data table. Don't forget to use the correct units.

Now return to your drawing of the floor plan. On the same grid, show *one* **of the following:**

- a sketch of one of your towers
- a cube model plan of one of your towers
- the top, front, and right side views of one of your towers

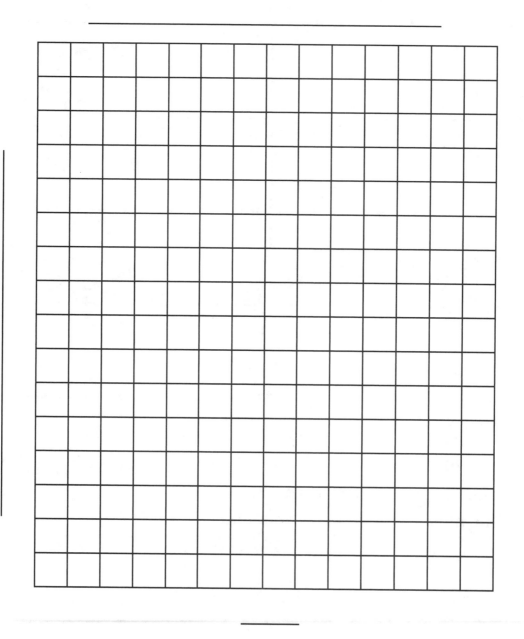

Make a point graph of your data. You will need to scale your graph so that you can make predictions about towers that have a height as tall as 20 cm and have a volume as large as 80 cc.

Explore

2. Describe any patterns you see in your data table.

3. A. Use your graph to predict the volume of a tower with your floor plan and a height of 12 centimeters. On your graph, show how you made your prediction.

   B. Check your prediction by finding the volume of the tower another way. Explain how you did this.

   C. Was your prediction a good one? _____ Why or why not?

4. If the mayor told you that the volume of your office tower could not be more than 80 cubic centimeters (cc), what is the tallest your tower

   could be? _____

   A. Solve this problem using your graph. Be sure the mayor can see how you used your graph to find the answer.

   B. Check your work by solving this problem another way. Explain how you did this.

5. The tallest office building in the United States is the Sears Tower in Chicago. It has 110 floors. If a tower with your floor plan had 110 floors, how many cubes would you need

to build the tower? _____

Show how you solved the problem.
Write a number sentence for this problem.

_____

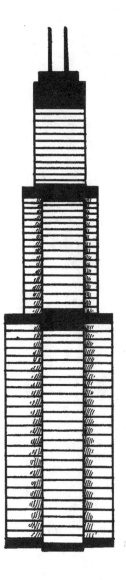

6. The final instructions tell your team that the volume of the office tower should be as close to 600 cc as possible. How tall will your office

tower be? _____ Show your work.

Tower Power

Toby and Tysha's Graph

Toby and Tysha are two architects in Tiny TIMS Town. They built towers and recorded data on the height and volume of their towers. Then they graphed their data on the same piece of graph paper.

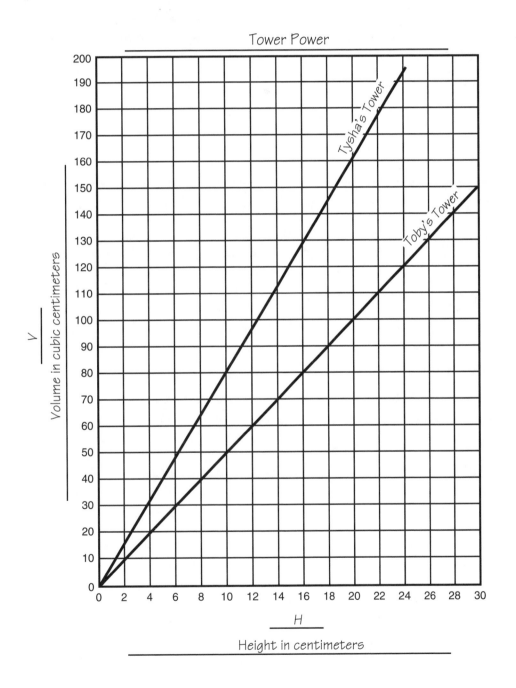

Use Toby and Tysha's graph to answer the following questions:

1. Toby built three towers with centimeter connecting cubes. He started to record his data. Fill in the data table completely.

Toby's Tower Power

H Height (in cm)	V Volume (in cc)
5 cm	
10 cm	
	100 cc

For Questions 2–8, find the answer and explain how you solved each problem.

2. What is the area of Toby's floor plan?

3. Toby wants to build a tower that is 30 cm tall. How many centimeter connecting cubes will he need?

4. Tysha built a tower 10 cm tall. What is the volume of her tower?

5. Tysha built a tower that is 15 cm tall. What is the volume of this tower?

6. Tysha built a tower which has a volume of 160 cc. How tall was this tower? Write a number sentence for this problem.

7. If Tysha has 100 centimeter connecting cubes, how high can her tower be?

8. Whose tower floor plan is larger, Toby's or Tysha's? Explain how you know.